THE SOCIOPATH'S GUIDE TO GETTING AHEAD

THE SOCIOPATH'S GUIDE TO GETTING AHEAD

TIPS FOR THE DARK ART OF MANIPULATION

~

P.T. ELLIOTT

Skyhorse Publishing

Skyhorse Publishing books may be purchased in bulk at special discounts for sales promotion, corporate gifts, fund-raising, or educational purposes. Special editions can also be created to specifications. For details, contact the Special Sales Department, Skyhorse Publishing, 307 West 36th Street, 11th Floor, New York, NY 10018 or info@skyhorsepublishing.com.

Skyhorse® and Skyhorse Publishing® are registered trademarks of Skyhorse Publishing, Inc.®, a Delaware corporation.

Visit our website at www.skyhorsepublishing.com.

10 9 8 7 6 5 4 3 2 1

Library of Congress Cataloging-in-Publication Data is available on file.

Cover design by Rain Saukas
Cover photo credit: iStock

Print ISBN: 978-1-5107-2538-6
Ebook ISBN: 978-1-5107-2539-3

Printed in the United States of America

I really do admire you a bit. You're an intelligent person of great moral character who has taken a very courageous stand. I'm an intelligent person with no moral character at all, so I'm in an ideal position to appreciate it.

—Joseph Heller, *Catch 22*

CONTENTS

Introduction   ix

Part One: **Getting In**   **1**
Chapter 1:   What They Think about You   3
Chapter 2:   Belief and Cognitive Bias   17
Chapter 3:   Jobs That Are Good for You   24
Chapter 4:   Acing the Interview   39
Chapter 5:   Personalities   60
Chapter 6:   Power   71

Part Two: **Getting Up**   **81**
Chapter 7:   Create an Effective Character   83
Chapter 8:   Disguise and Recharge   93
Chapter 9:   Low-Hanging Fruit   104
Chapter 10:   Allies   112
Chapter 11:   Pressure   116
Chapter 12:   Enemies   136
Chapter 13:   You Versus You   143
Chapter 14:   Winning   146

Epilogue   157
Thanks   158
Selected Bibliography   159
Endnotes   161

INTRODUCTION

I'm resourceful . . . I'm creative, I'm young, unscrupulous, highly motivated, highly skilled. In essence what I'm saying is that society cannot afford to lose me. I am an asset.

—Bret Easton Ellis, *American Psycho*

A re you a sociopath in the office, feeling trapped? Feeling vulnerable and exposed? It's to be expected. Because right now it's dangerous to be you. The proliferation of safe spaces, delicate snowflakes, and the "prosocial" culture encroaching on many work environments may require you to curb your ruthless instincts more carefully than ever before. The alarming increase in support for introverts and sensitives in society threaten your natural, simple, "greed is good" approach to business. While some people proudly proclaim they are not politically correct, don't be fooled. The increased demand for prosocial behavior is not an arbitrary trend, nor is it likely to slink away, because more than 80 percent of US jobs are now service jobs. And service jobs require repeated customer interaction[1] and satisfaction. This means even the most ferocious, infantile, fussy, stingy, and irritating customer must be "pleased" and consider you to be friendly, courteous, and efficient . . . or else they'll hit the red frown button at the exit or excoriate you with zero stars and a huffy review on Yelp. Yes, this is where we now live. Consumers can hold you hostage and destroy business with unfair ease. Social scientists bent on exposing the dark side of charisma[2] have HR ladies creaming in their jeans over their conveniently touchy-feely findings, and growing expectations for this kind of surface-level niceness really puts a cramp in your style.

At the same time, you are more famous and popular than ever. This is your second problem. Exposure. People want to be like you because you aren't afraid to take what you want. In fact, you could argue the entire "how to get ahead" branch of the self-help industry is designed to enable "normal" people to behave like sociopaths, even while claiming that it can all be done while still being a good person. Your secret coping and manipulation mechanisms are constantly being studied and copied move for move. The new, "scientifically grounded" insights these books cite in abundance are in reality fantastic tips for perfecting the art of manipulation—and that's your territory. This book will help hone your natural skills and innate understanding to beat out those who are trying this behavior on for size, but lack your amoral fortitude and preternatural calm under pressure.

In our current political situation, you are going to be studied, discussed, and aped more than ever before. President Trump uses many of the psychological tools described in this book to great effect. He understands embodied cognition (using posture to express power), confirmation bias (people seeking out a loud expression of what they already believe), cognitive dissonance (ignoring contradictory ideas and uncertainty), halo effect (assuming that a good businessman will be a good leader), and bias (relying on stereotypes). All of which will be discussed in the following pages.

It's also good to be you.

Unfettered by fear or a sense of guilt, you can reclaim these tools and use them in ways only a true sociopath can in order to get in on the secret these books always promise, the dark beating heart at the core of the self-help movement: *How to get want you want because you want it . . . no matter what (or who) stands in your way.* Here's the rub. It's impossible for everyone to get what they want, just because they want it. As soon as two people want the same thing, you're already at an impasse. Luckily, you're not weighed down by a conscience which might stop others from doing crummy things to people to get what they want. Advantage, sociopath. Just like the con who understands that he can work a mark by lending his own confidence, you too can manipulate the emotions and motivations of others in order to get what you want, instead of what they want. Using the latest in social psychology, cognitive science, and social economics, we are going to remind you how.

If you are a sociopath and not in jail, it's because at a young age you realized you are someone special who needs to tread carefully and hide your true nature in order to survive.

Dale Carnegie really opened up the art of how to get what you want with his famous book *How to Win Friends and Influence People* widely read and admired by millions and he did it in the nicest possible way. Even so, maybe his most arresting pupil was Charles Manson. Manson studied Carnegie in prison at a self-help class arming Manson with the simple idea that the most effective way to get someone to do something you want them to do is to make them think it's something they wanted to do themselves.[3] This bit of powerful advice enabled Manson to overcome his petty criminal carjacker fate and become leader of the insanely dark and influential sex-death cult, the Manson Family. (US penal system, betcha didn't see that one coming.)

As sociopaths, you know a lot of this stuff intuitively, but it's time for you to up your game and take your evolutionary advantage one step further. Intended for sociopaths ranging from those running an honest business to the street thug looking to become criminal mastermind, this book will help you find ways of getting ahead without getting caught. It is designed to help you navigate the current work environment in a way that is maximally beneficial to *YOU*, without resorting to the classic behaviors you have used in the past. Following the tips in this book could mean the difference between prison and promotion.

PART ONE

GETTING IN

CHAPTER 1
WHAT THEY THINK ABOUT YOU

If that's true—if you don't know who I am—then maybe your best course would be to *tread lightly*.

—Walter White, *Breaking Bad*

You're familiar with the terms. Employed frequently and freely, their popular meanings are sloppy yet evocative: sociopath, psychopath, narcissist, Machiavellian, antisocial, maladjusted, disordered, pathological, incorrigible, malevolent, amoral asshole, con, degenerate, bad seed, blackhearted, rogue, creeper, psycho. Dark, nasty words they don't teach at charm school. Even the ancient Greeks named you "the unscrupulous."[1] You've been called many things, but let's face it, you don't actually care.

You don't naturally waste time with feelings except when trying to fathom the feelings of others in order to take control. Being called names doesn't really hurt your feelings, because you don't really have any serious feelings to begin with. To be a successful sociopath, you need to know who people imagine you are in order to effectively conceal yourself. You are not safe unless you learn to be a master deceiver. This is why we will start here: with you, and the telltale indicators used by shrinks, neuroscientists, journalists, and other nosy jerks to sniff you out.

If nothing else, always remember this: *better things come to he who remains hidden*.

Over the past twenty years, both the American population at large and corporate culture in particular have grown increasingly sociopathic.[2] Narcissism is up and empathy is down, which means you are in *style*. People are fascinated by you. Your darkest kind are like criminal rock stars, populating the television waves in endless crime dramas and historical reenactments with mesmeric, chilling verve. People believe your brightest kind are fearless creatures who run countries, command billions, and carelessly snort coke and chant heartily while beating their chests in crowded Wall Street restaurants. Everyone is obsessed with you.[3] Now get over it. While it may be flattering that so many people have taken an interest in you, it also draws unwanted attention and scrutiny. Never bring up sociopaths, never compare yourself to one, even if in the moment it will make you seem "cool." It's not worth it.

That said, the most famous and notorious of your kind—ruthless despots, serial killers, cult leaders—are in fact working in your favor. The more visible and outlandish these sociopaths are, the more their behavior provides cover for you. Their extreme, brutal, and exotic nature will seem so very different from yours. You seem to be a relative bore and should keep it that way.

Many estimate one in a hundred Americans is a sociopath, while others put the number closer to one in twenty-five and "much more common" in men than women.[4] On this front, a reasonably accepted figure is one woman to every three men.[5] We'll talk about why there is so much discrepancy in these numbers later, but based on any of these accounts, you are legion. Your top members are extremely successful, some reports show 3 to 4 percent of senior business positions are held by psychopaths[6] while others show a massively skewed *20 percent* of CEOs are psychopaths.[7] Before you say I told you so, also understand your percentage of the population in the criminal justice system is similarly skewed to at least sixteen percent sociopath.[8] Given the massive number of people in the penal system, that suggests that as many as 93 percent of male sociopaths are in prison or on parole.[9] That's a shit-ton of you guys. Your success window is small, so you really do need to learn to play your cards right. It's a dangerous world for you.

> "We're the one percenters, man—the one percent that don't fit and don't care."—A Hell's Angel speaking for the permanent record.
>
> —Hunter S. Thompson, *Hell's Angels*

If you want to be difficult and go rooting through all the available statistics, you'll be able to find studies crunching out different results, because here's the genius behind the sociopath label: no one can agree on exactly *who* you are. Some argue "psychopaths don't exist at all and asking them to define *psychopath* [is] like asking them to define a nervous breakdown."[10] Jon Ronson, author of *The Psychopath Test*, says, "You shouldn't define people by their maddest edges. And what Tony is, is he's a semi-psychopath. He's a gray area in a world that doesn't like gray areas. But the gray areas are where you find the complexity. It's where you find the humanity, and it's where you find the truth."[11] So what *is* a sociopath, exactly? Inexactitude and disagreement regarding your temperament provides a perfect alibi should you ever be accused of being a "fucking psycho" and need to defend yourself. Two words will do: *Prove it.*

Amid this confusion is the million-dollar question: Are sociopaths really becoming more prevalent? Are our breeding habits and capitalistic culture spawning more of you? Or are we diluting the brand by calling people sociopaths more easily and letting them into the club?

ACCORDING TO THE EXPERTS

Psychologists, neuroscientists, and others have been attempting to describe and diagnose your mercurial inner state with more precision for years. Psychopath is derived from the Greek words psyche or "mind" and pathos or "suffering," a pan-directional screwed-up-in-the-head term that's so general it's practically meaningless. All humans are screwed up in the head in one way or another. In the late 1800s, French doctor Philippe Pinel renamed your "condition" *manie sans delire*, or "mania without delusion," meaning to describe you as being without moral restraint or emotionally insane, yet able conduct yourself without shouting at shadows and gibbering at walls. Intellectually sound, yet emotionally damaged. Now it's getting interesting.

In England, the Victorians blamed the perceived increase of this condition on industrialization, capitalism, and the decline of religion. In America during the temperance and moral-hygiene movements, psychopathy was seen as a vice caused by degeneracy—a kind of societal disease or moral depravity. Today, the "without delusion" portion of Pinel's description is considered a proper definition of being sane, and criminals who are deemed psychopaths by the court generally cannot plead not guilty by reason of insanity. "Psychopathic killers . . . are not mad, according to accepted legal and psychiatric standards."[12]

OPEN A CAN OF WORMS

If you need to get a runaway conversation back under your control, there's nothing like the little prick of expansive questioning to deflate some lecturing know-it-all full of hot air and certitude. In this case, a fun line of questioning might go something like this:

You: "Ha, yeah, it's always fun to see how accepted norms of proper and illegal behavior have slid all around over time. I mean, cocaine used to be legal and whores had no right to vote. What exactly is a "societal disease" anyway? What does it mean? And who decides? And who chooses those deciders? Is it a government thing, a church thing, a jail thing, or a hospital thing? Does this mean society gets to call behavior it doesn't like a disease? Clearly it has in the past . . ."

In 1928, Sigmund Freud circled around a pretty modern description of yourself:

Two traits are essential in a criminal: boundless egoism and a strong destructive urge. Common to both of these, and a necessary condition for their expression, is absence of love, lack of an emotional appreciation of (human) objects.[13]

But he left it at that. In the 1930s people started calling you sociopaths, just to mix it up a bit. In 1941, psychiatrist Hervey Cleckley rerouted the concept of "psychopath" toward defining you as having an aggressive mindset intent on pursuing "vivid patterns of maladjustment" which inevitably lead to criminality and disorder. In his book *Mask of Sanity* he describes a psychopath as "a biologic organism outwardly intact, showing excellent peripheral function, but centrally deficient or disabled in such a way that abilities . . . cannot be utilized consistently for sane purposes or prevented from regularly working toward self-destructive and other seriously pathologic results."[14] We'll keep "excellent peripheral function," thank you. But Cleckley was apparently unaware of the large numbers of successful sociopaths in society. He underestimated the breadth and versatility of his subject.

Cleckley clarified his position in 1964, describing you as having:

> . . . superficial charm and good intelligence: absence of delusions and other signs of irrational thinking; absence of "nervousness" or other psychoneurotic manifestations; unreliability, untruthfulness, and insincerity; lack of remorse or shame; inadequately motivated antisocial behavior; poor judgement and failure to learn by experience; pathologic egocentricity and incapacity for love; general poverty in major affective reactions; specific loss of insight; unresponsiveness in general interpersonal relations; fantastic and uninviting behavior with drink and sometimes without; suicide rarely carried out; sex life impersonal, trivial, and poorly integrated; and failure to follow any life plan.[15]

In 1993, psychologist Robert D. Hare got more precise in his book *Without Conscience* where he identified six emotional/interpersonal traits often present in psychopaths:

- glib and superficial (charm)
- egocentric and grandiose
- lack of remorse or guilt
- lack of empathy
- deceitful and manipulative
- shallow emotions

And six expressions of social deviance:

- impulsive
- poor behavior controls
- need for excitement
- lack of responsibility
- early behavior problems
- adult antisocial behavior[16]

If you don't live in a cave and have ever surfed the net for articles about yourself, you already know this. So I'll keep it brief. Hare created the Psychopathy Checklist or "PCL-R" to score a person's level or degree of psychopathy. In addition to these traits, the twenty-part checklist includes:

- Pathological lying
- Parasitic lifestyle
- Promiscuous sexual behavior
- Early behavior problems
- Lack of realistic long-term goals
- Many short-term marital relationships
- Revocation of conditional release
- Criminal versatility[17]

Typically used by law enforcement shrinks, the Psychopathy Checklist requires a licensed professional to understand how to "read" a person's character. Your score is based on their ranking of each trait. Zero: does not apply. One: applies somewhat. Two: applies fully. Meaning the possible scores range from zero to forty. Clearly, scoring a two on many of these would not look good for you. But once again, Hare has focused on the criminal subgroup. His test may work great in prison once you've already been busted, and don't have as much at stake in hiding yourself. But if you are still on the outside, you know how to be more careful. Hare himself said "If I weren't studying psychopaths in prison, I'd do it at the stock exchange."[18] Well, why doesn't he go to Wall Street? He admits it's because that would be difficult: "Prisoners are easy. They like meeting researchers. It breaks up the monotony of their day. But CEOs, politicians..."[19]

You've heard the phrase "on the spectrum" used to deride an awkward-to-obsessive colleague or even just a weird mouth breather. It's meant to pin the subject somewhere on the autism spectrum between mild and Rain Man. Many feel "psychos" similarly exist on a spectrum, with the "successful" sociopath falling somewhere around the twenty-point mark on the Hare checklist score. Neuroscientist and self-diagnosed psychopath James Fallon says, "I believe there's a sweet spot on the psychopathy spectrum. People who are

twenty-five or thirty on the Hare scale are dangerous, but we need a lot of twenties around—people with the chutzpah and brio and outrageousness to keep humanity vibrant and adaptable—and alive."[20]

The *Diagnostic and Statistical Manual of Mental Disorders* (*DSM-V*) officially describes your condition very broadly under the umbrella of "Antisocial Personality Disorder," which is "a pervasive pattern of disregard for and violation of the rights of others."

Talk about pussyfooting around. You don't even get your own category. These guys don't want to commit to saying anything decisive just yet.[21] And again, this diagnosis focuses on people caught doing destructive and illegal activity. The successful, functional sociopath is not included, pointing out there is yet to be an agreed-upon underlying "disease" that can be diagnosed without the presentation of socially maladaptive symptoms. All these famous studies focus only on those of you who've ended up in the big house. What about Wall Street and the White House? No matter. Leave them to their circular logic and limited vision; at least you know who they think you are.

SPECIAL CASE: NARCISSIST.

Of *course* you're a special case, because you're a narcissist. You're not a run-of-the-mill sociopath. You're obsessed with getting attention and approval from others. You have your own *DSM-V* entry. You need to be liked and admired as if all of life is one long-running seventh-grade popularity contest. With so many of your other traits indistinguishable from those of the sociopath, I feel this book will be useful to you. I'll leave your need for attention and "Feed the Hole" hunger for constant validation at the gate and suggest you look elsewhere for advice on how to get your ego stroked. But the rest of your personality should find much useful here. Like I said, this book isn't here to draw descriptive lines in the mental sand but to focus on the problem of getting ahead. So please join us. I promise to point out a few things you are really good at along the way, so the regular socio-joe can learn from you, too.

There has been much semantic wrestling over you as clinicians attempt to parse the broad description of sociopathy into separately named conditions. For example, the "Dark Triad" tries to separate narcissists from psychopaths from Machiavellian types by highlighting a few distinct traits. Others separate psychopaths as those who respond aggressively to physical threat from narcissists who respond aggressively to ego threat.[22] Some study nature-versus-nurture, claiming that sociopaths were created by abuse while psychopaths are genetically compromised.[23] Could there be true distinctions? Sure. But they're minor details compared to the large, dark core you all share.

While psychologists have been working on definitions and semantics, neuroscientists have also been studying possible physical manifestations of psychopathy and are beginning to define who's who by mapping reduced neural activity and abnormalities in the limbic system.[24] One of the lead researchers in this field, James Fallon, inadvertently discovered that his own brain scan contained these same psychopathic abnormalities. His friends and family readily agreed with the diagnosis but his behavior had been noncriminal and highly functional his entire life.

So where does that leave us? Like "crazy" or "brilliant," sociopathy is a mental state which has thus far eluded a definitive, concrete, pathological diagnosis. You are a complicated creature. In defense of the shrinks, this circles back to the problem of differentiating between psychological and physiological origins. Does getting abused as a child affect your limbic system? If you have a normal brain yet pass the maladaptive personality tests with flying colors, are you still a real sociopath? What if you have the abnormal brain but act like a sweetheart? Fuck it. You don't really care. But these are all interesting questions you can tap dance around with to keep other people from pinning you down.

TRUE CONFESSIONS

"I don't need to recover from anything. I am recovered. I'm a twenty-first century man. You see, inside all of us there is the old brain, the emotional brain, full of fear and nervousness. But wrapped around that old brain is the new mind: the rational, thinking, planning, cool modern mind. This new mind grew as humans evolved into more complex beings with more advanced societies. This new mind is a further step in evolution from the old brain, man. It is more advanced. In the sociopath, the old brain has been more effectively crushed and inhibited by this new mind than in regular people. Like a rabbit in the boa constrictor's embrace, the new mind is squeezing out the old brain. It's a further step in evolution. Eventually the new mind will squeeze out the old brain altogether. This is why sociopaths are actually the most advanced humans on the planet."

—James Dewitt, stock trader. New York City

There's *always* an agenda. Everyone has their reason (and grant application) for pursuing category classifications and definitions to try to concretely define your mind or separate you into smaller and smaller subgroups. But we're not going to help them. For the purposes of this book, from now on you're all "sociopaths." If you're an expert reading this in your tiny windowless office and getting angry, I advise you to either get over it or put the book down. This book is not for you. It's for sociopaths and other smart people who are here for a little learning, fun, and profit.

Maybe think of diagnosing a sociopath as like diagnosing an alcoholic. There are hospitalized alcoholics, self-proclaimed tragic alcoholics, functional secret alcoholics, alcoholic disasters, alcohol-fueled geniuses, and heavy drinkers who don't give a shit one way or another what you call them. Anyone who tries to pigeonhole one into a particular category is as likely to get agreement as a beer bottle in the face. Similarly, maybe there are criminal sociopaths, personal-life-in-shambles sociopaths, functional sociopaths, charismatic genius sociopaths, and none-of-your-fucking-business sociopaths.

ON DEFENSE

Remember, every insult can be turned into a backhanded compliment with a gentle shift of vocabulary. Impulsive? Try: unencumbered. Kevin Dutton puts a useful positive spin on Hare's psychopathic traits, calling them in part "charisma, focus, mental toughness, fearlessness, mindfulness, action, self-confidence, and coolness under pressure."[25] Feel free to use these terms to correct anyone who's trying to deride you. You can also point out that Hemingway's definition of courage itself was "grace under pressure."[26]

In 1977, Cathy Widom, a researcher looking for noncriminal psychopaths in Boston came up with these want ads, which also makes you sound pretty good:

ARE YOU ADVENTUROUS?
Psychologist studying adventurous carefree people who've led exciting impulsive lives. If you're the kind of person who'd do almost anything for a dare and want to participate in a paid experiment, send name, address, phone, and short biography proving how interesting you are . . .

WANTED: charming, aggressive, carefree people who are impulsively irresponsible but are good at handling people and at looking after number one.[27]

Finally, Hare interviewed a psychopath who was not impressed with the checklist wording, at all. He offered these much more positive interpretations; this is the kind of spin that will get you places:

> *Glib and superficial*—"What is negative about articulation skills?"
> *Egocentric and grandiose*—"How can I attain something if I don't reach high?"
> *Deceitful and manipulative*—"All of us are manipulative to some degree. Isn't positive manipulation common?"
> *Impulsive*—"Can be associated with creativity, living in the now, being spontaneous and free."
> *Poor behavioral controls*—"Violent and aggressive outbursts may be a defensive mechanism, a false front, a tool for survival in a jungle."
> *Need for excitement*—"Courage to reject the routine, monotonous, or uninteresting. Living on the edge, doing things that are risky, exciting, challenging, living life to its fullest, being alive rather than dull, boring, and almost dead."[28]

YOU ARE LEGENDARY

One of the most powerful ways you can manipulate others is through belief. Belief is the essential force you need to understand and appreciate to make this book work for you. We'll come back to this in depth later on, but for now, let's look at what average people believe about you. How you react to these common beliefs will be far more consequential to your success than any definition, statistic, or checklist.

BELIEF: *You make a great first impression.*
　　True. In psychological tests, people scoring high on Machiavellian tendencies make significant and pervasive good impressions. Viewers are more likely to describe High Machs as "clever, bold, ambitious, dominating, persuasive, confident, relaxed, and talented" while describing Low Machs as "cowardly, indecisive, gullible, insecure, emotional, and unintelligent." And people like the High Machs more.[29] It is this fact—that sociopaths often make fantastic

first impressions—that some experts find to be "one of the most troubling findings in all of psychology."[30] Bravo, *but . . .*

It's extremely important not to let this go to your head, and here's why. The effect of this initial "glow" tends to wear off faster than you might think. In one study, after as little as two and a half hours[31] of exposure, subjects who at first had a positive impression of narcissists began to negatively perceive them as "self-enhancers." You need to guard the glow of your first impression. Don't get me wrong, self-enhancement can get you far, but you need to be subtle about it. You should regard this first-impression advantage as something like starting a track race in the sixth lane. You begin way out ahead, but once you round the turn, people catch up, and catch on, unless you really know how to run.

How to handle it: Concentrate on preserving a good impression over the longer term by resisting the urge to show off once you get the gig. If you do need to preen and be a peacock about it go do it in an empty parking lot or someplace where no one can see you, and get it out of your system. (Feel free to also use this parking lot escape when you are sorely tested and tempted to punch someone in the face.)

BELIEF: *You don't feel emotions and lack empathy.*

True to a greater or lesser degree, depending on how sociopathic you are. You don't care about other people. That you don't feel emotion is a fact which is important to keep to yourself. Even if you strongly agree with certain statements from diagnostic tests, you should never *admit* that to anyone. For example, "Rate from one to five (one=strongly disagree to five=strongly agree) 'Success is based on survival of the fittest; I am not concerned about the losers.' or 'People who are stupid enough to get ripped off usually deserve it.'"[32] If these questions aren't already obviously leading and dangerous enough to make you choke on your beer, you need to learn. No matter what you really think, never agree to clumsy and entrapping statements such as these.

How to handle it: Avoid cold or superior language. Don't refer to a person as "pathetic" or a horrible accident as "fascinating." Try to avoid being outwardly mean. Take the online test at http://personality-testing.info/tests/

LSRP.php and see if you can score a five in both primary and secondary psychopathy. Then never publicly agree with or repeat any of the statements you "strongly agreed" to, ever again.

BELIEF: *You have a hard time reading emotions in others.*

Mostly False. While you don't feel emotion yourself, you find it fascinating in others and expend a great deal of effort learning to recognize and copy emotional expression. While there is some evidence you aren't great at noting expressions of fear,[33] many tests show you are a good study and show no impairment in recognizing an emotion in others.[34]

How to handle it: Keep up the good work. Correctly identifying the emotional state of another person is essential for effective manipulation. The more closely you can align your reaction to their mood, the more likely they will accept what you say.

BELIEF: *You don't suffer from guilt.*

> People incapable of guilt usually do have a good time.
>
> —Rust Cohle, *True Detective*

True, but guilt isn't likely to be something HR is looking for when they're kicking your tires and checking under the hood. They'll more likely be looking for aggression, agreeableness, reliability, and fact checking your competence. We'll get back to your lack of guilt later, once you're established and can really put it to good use.

BELIEF: *You are more intelligent than most people.*

False. Sorry to say this, but if scientific tests are to be trusted, this is not the case. Across the population, your IQ is neither higher nor lower on average than everyone else's.[35] But that doesn't matter, you're not working for an IQ test, but for malleable, biased people who will most likely perceive you as more intelligent because you feel that way yourself and aren't afraid to show it. Keep up the good work. If you're not good at something, just pretend you are. This may be stressful to some, but you'll be fine. Remember this: projecting confidence literally cannot be overestimated.

Everybody says things like "fake it till you make it" and "confidence trumps competence," and they are absolutely true. Studies show people who act like they know what they are talking about, even if they don't and are completely wrong in their assertions, are viewed as being literally as good at that something as someone who actually knows what he's doing.[36] This astonishing fact is yours for the using. And in this post-truth era where fact checking is a useless pastime for nerds, it's only going to get better from here. The secret is to assert with confidence while keeping the topics broad and steering the conversation away from the other person's expertise. Asserting yourself blindly in someone else's wheelhouse can lead to mistakes that will blow your cover.

How to handle it: Just keep acting like you know what you're doing,

BELIEF: *You feel entitled.*

True. You do think you're better than others and deserve more. But who's gonna give it to you unless you ask for it?! Exceptionalism applies to you!

BELIEF: *You have no inner self.*

It's complicated.

CHAPTER 2

BELIEF AND COGNITIVE BIAS

Belief is nearly the whole of the universe whether based on truth or not.

—Kurt Vonnegut Jr., *Bluebeard*

No matter how rational, reasonable, or logical someone claims to be, human beings rarely make decisions based on facts. They never have. People make decisions despite the facts, based on what they believe. For you to be effective, it's essential to understand belief and how it works in everyday operation. Harnessing belief is the most powerful tool you have to manipulate others. Harnessing their belief, that is, not yours. This power cannot be overestimated and is worth repeating as a core tenet of this book:

Exploiting another's belief is the *most powerful tool* you have to get what you want.

While not qualitatively different from belief in God or aliens, belief itself shouldn't be sidelined as a conception of "religious experience." You need to start thinking about belief as resulting from pervasive thought processes you constantly rely on for countless mundane decisions every day. Which cereal to buy? Which is better: non-GMO, organic, sugar-free, gluten-free, fat-free, on sale? What's fact, what's fad? The truth may not be available or conclusive, or you may have more important things to worry about. So you buy a cereal you remember your dad liked. It's pretty good, so you buy it again, because you bought it last time. Then it becomes your favorite. And then it becomes the *best*.

People come to believe something in one of two basic ways. Either through direct experience ("I saw it with my own eyes") or by what an authority tells them ("It must be true. General Gris reported it to the *New York Times*"). Which one the person relies on is largely consistent and based on their personality. Once formed, beliefs will be retained, accessed, and acted upon repeatedly as a reliable source. This doesn't mean beliefs can't change. Clearly, they do all the time. But it takes special skill to change others' beliefs to suit your needs.

When attempting to foment a belief, it's most effective to present the subject with the belief-generating material he generally prefers. To the direct experience person, show hard evidence, test results, samples, pictures, proofs. For the person who accepts authority, tell them the boss or God said it was so. Then leave them alone to ponder it for themselves. Belief helps them decide what to do. Alongside experience and authority, COGNITIVE BIAS helps them decide what to believe.

COGNITIVE BIAS

Cognitive bias describes the pervasive tendency human beings have to latch on to specific kinds of information in order to form beliefs, even if the results may be illogical, unfounded, and otherwise insane. Even if it leads to mistakes in judgement about what is true or ultimately beneficial. And it will. But if it doesn't hurt us, if it's "good" for us in the moment, our minds don't care whether it's true or prudent. Our brains are constantly solving the problem of living with what's called a HEURISTIC approach: if it's practical and sufficient in the near term, that's good enough. It doesn't have to be perfect, just handy. Biases are a quick mental shorthand evolved to steer us toward safety and survival, not truth. They also control how we remember things and reinforce lasting world views.

You are not immune. You also rely on cognitive bias all the time. While it's super-useful to exploit the cognitive bias in others, you'll be better off if you can do as much rational, cold, hard, logical thinking as you can possibly stand. Try to be truthful with yourself about your own biases. This can help you steer clear of traps set by others. Reflect the beliefs of people around you back to them, liberally, as your own. It will make them like you. Don't admit your real beliefs to anybody; they will use it against you, eventually. Remember, you may be the only sociopath in the room but you're not the only one trying to influence others in order to get their way.

When you feel pressure, ask yourself, "Is this person using what I believe to push me into a corner?" Then, "If I change this belief, will it get me out of a jam?" If the answer is "yes," focus on changing your mind, rather than defending your position. This is another (underused) heuristic approach which is not perfect, but useful and expedient. If you can remember it's about getting what you want, not defending what you believe, things will be infinitely easier for you.

There are hundreds of biases that have been tested and verified, from the fact that people generally like things to stay the same to the fact they overestimate distances when looking down. (Fear of falling is adaptively protective.) While we're not here to explore all the cognitive biases out there, we will expose many throughout this book when it's useful for you to exploit a bias and manipulate belief by making something "handy."

With the risk of dating myself, I'll illustrate a few below with quotes from Donald Trump, who drums up bias with preternatural ease, and whose stunning statements you will surely remember.

CONFIRMATION BIAS. People seek, value, believe, and remember information that supports their preexisting beliefs. At the same time, they tend to doubt, discount, forget, and ignore anything that contradicts these beliefs,[1] a kind of factual cherry-picking. Even when it is dangerous to do so. The incredible power of confirmation bias underscores the importance of belief. Here's an example from Trump of confirmation bias in action: *"Well, someone's doing the raping . . . I mean, somebody's doing it. Who's doing the raping? Who's doing the raping?"* (Mexicans are criminals and rapists). As part of confirmation bias, people also see ambiguous evidence as supporting their point of view, and will hold on to beliefs even in the face of contradictory evidence.

ATTRIBUTION BIAS (sometimes called **SELF-SERVING BIAS**). People tend to believe they are solely responsible for their accomplishments and other people or external factors are responsible for their failures. Another Trump example: *"If we went and got the single greatest health-care plan in the history of the world, we would not get one Democrat vote, because they're* *obstructionists. . . . If we had even a little Democrat support, just a little, like a couple of votes, you'd have everything."*

UNREALISTIC OPTIMISM. People have an overinflated idea of where they stand in the world in relation to both chance and statistics. They believe they are more likely to win the lottery and less likely to have a heart attack than the numbers and laws of the universe suggest. Example: *"We will have so much winning if I get elected that you may get bored with winning. Believe me."*

HALO EFFECT. People assume that if someone has one good quality, then they will have lots of other positive qualities, explains social psychologist Heidi Grant Halvorson, even if there is no actual correlation: "If you are handsome

or charming, people will assume you are probably smart and trustworthy, too."[2] Etcetera. Example: *"I'm really rich . . . And by the way, I'm not even saying that in a braggadocio . . . that's the kind of thinking you need for this country."*

Throughout this book, we will look at ways to activate and encourage bias in others when it is useful to do so.

Humans will fall back on a belief, once formed, because it's easier. One of the core findings of social psychology is the fact that people are mentally lazy. They rarely if ever reason something through step-by-step from the beginning to the end. If they did, they'd never get out of the house. Halvorson calls us "cognitive misers [who] think only as much as they feel they need to, and no more."[3] We rely on previously formed beliefs, decisions, and pathways whenever possible to preserve energy. Even the scientific method herself is subject to cognitive bias. The convention is, the simpler and more elegant the explanation is, the more probably true. This may be the case, or it may be all that we can handle. This is known as OCCAM'S RAZOR and gives you an unexpected opening. Keep it simple and you are more likely to be believed. Like blinkers on a racehorse blocking out all the peripheral spectacle and narrowing the horse's vision to just that one piece of track ahead, cognitive biases are thought to be a successful adaptation to keep you from getting lost in the infinite, fractured, bright beautiful world.

MEMORY BIAS

MEMORY BIAS is a whole subcategory with many individual biases. Memory will influence belief, both as things are happening and long after they have passed.

ILLUSORY TRUTH EFFECT. An amazing memory bias where "repeating a statement makes it seem more likely to be true."[4] The statement becomes familiar. It is remembered. So repeat yourself. *Repeat yourself.* People find statements that have been repeated as more valid or true than things they have heard just for the first time. Because they sound familiar. And "because of the way our minds work, what is familiar is also true. Familiar things require less effort to process and that feeling of ease unconsciously signals truth."[5] This is called COGNITIVE FLUENCY. So repeat yourself.

Wearing white increases your odds of winning an argument. Naw. I'm just fucking with you. I don't have any evidence for that. But simply because I said it, some of you will half-remember this "fact" in a year and repeat it with confidence to someone you're trying to impress at the bar. Because you remember it. Sometime down the line, you *will* subconsciously select a white shirt because you read this. This is predictable. I just inserted the seeds of fallacy into your worldview which some of you will come to believe is true, just because I said it. See how easy that is? Wearing white increases your odds of winning an argument. There. I said it again, so the seed is now bigger. You're welcome.

HINDSIGHT BIAS. People come to believe an event was predictable after the fact.[6] As in "I knew it all along." When they didn't. When they couldn't. This is sometimes known as creeping determinism. As in, "Looking back on it, he understood with creeping determinism that he knew the plane was going to crash all along." How does the sociopath exploit this fun thing? I don't know right now. If you figure it out, let me know and I'll say, "Exactly. That's what I always said." Okay, so you get the idea. We'll discuss other memory biases as they come up. This is just to give you a flavor of how memory relates to belief.

But wait, it gets even weirder. In time, the more pressure placed on a belief, the more arguments against it, the more emotional it becomes, the more dearly this belief is held. Even in the face of overwhelming contrary evidence, people will stand by their belief, because they believe it. As Francis Bacon wrote, "The human understanding when it has once adopted an opinion ... draws all things else to support and agree with it. And though there be a greater number and weight of instances to be found on the other side, yet these it either neglects or despises, or else by some distinction sets aside or rejects."

Since you don't possess empathy, the mysterious art of winning people over is often beyond you. But knowing that people rely heavily on cognitive bias to get through even the most mundane daily operations will enable you to manipulate them more easily. People rely on what they know. They're paying less attention than you might think. They're thinking less than you expect. They're often careless and sloppy. They remember conservatively and selectively. Played the right way, these appalling lapses of attention and alertness give you an advantage. This may be the most important tool you will come away with from this book: how to manipulate belief in others by recognizing and exploiting their cognitive biases.

CHAPTER 3

JOBS THAT ARE GOOD FOR YOU

The new tech industry is populated by young, amoral hustlers, the kind of young guys . . . who watched *The Social Network* and its depiction of Mark Zuckerberg as a lying, thieving, backstabbing prick—and left the theater wanting to be just like that guy.

—Dan Lyons, *Disrupted: My Misadventure in the Start-Up Bubble*

You tend to be gamblers[1] and are attracted to companies that are in on the action. The faster paced the better, with high risk and higher profit.[2] You operate best in jobs with little regimented structure or enforced routine. There's no better place than a shop run on barely contained chaos for you to show off your preternatural ability to remain calm and confident. Your slow, even pulse in the face of general panic will make you look like a hero, while the disorganization all around will enable you to maneuver, exploit loopholes, and avoid getting trapped or exposed. When in doubt, keep moving.

Partially for this reason, you like cities. They are easy to hide in. Cities are also exciting and fun for you. Bob Hare said, "Psychopaths tend to gravitate toward the bright lights. You'll find lots of them in New York and London and Los Angeles."[3] So pack your bags and get out of the boonies for starters.

As psychologist Paul Babiak writes, "When dramatic organizational change is added to the normal levels of job insecurity, personality clashes, and political battling, the resulting *chaotic milieu* provides both the necessary stimulation and sufficient cover for psychopathic behavior. . . . Rapid business growth, increased downsizing, frequent reorganizations, mergers, acquisitions, and joint ventures have inadvertently increased the number of attractive employment opportunities"[4] for you. Start-ups, mergers, and firms touting a creative approach to management are good places to start. Others might call this type of organization shambolic, chaotic, disorganized, or confused. But you'll settle in just fine.

Look for loosely defined jobs with potential for advancement and variety. It helps to choose something you are also naturally good at, because while competence alone is completely overrated when climbing the ladder is concerned, it is a decent way to avoid scrutiny.

Everything will be easier for you if you are actually somewhat good at what you do.

TECH

Tech start-ups are obviously the unicorn in the room. With rapidly changing technology affecting every aspect of modern life, investors still crazy to find the next Facebook will throw money at a company named after an animal which doesn't exist. A unicorn company is defined as a private start-up thought to be worth at least a billion dollars. Importantly, this valuation is based on revenue levels, not the actual profits and losses of the company, which are legally kept private until the IPO is announced and the papers are filed. It's only then that the investors can see what kind of animal comes out of the egg. This is heaven for you.

Except . . . you won't be alone. Much of the valley is playing by your rules. Reporter Dan Lyons, who did hard time there, describes the new business model like this:

> Grow fast, lose money, go public . . . It's a simple racket. Venture capitalists pump millions of dollars into a company. The company spends some of that money coding up a "minimum viable product," or MVP[5] . . . and then pumps enormous sums into acquiring customers. . . . The losses pile up, but the revenue number rises. . . . There's also a sense among start-ups that it's okay for them to break the rules because they're underdogs competing against huge opponents; they're David, firing his slingshot at Goliath. Another argument is that the big guys break just as many rules as the little guys. Everybody cheats, and only

suckers drive inside the lines. . . . The whole thing is based on companies trying to achieve escape velocity before they blow themselves up.[6]

These are all plans and rationalizations that suit you very well. Your ability to talk a big game will be an asset, the frenetic pace is stimulating, it should all be great good fun, and you could make a killing if the company goes public and doesn't implode.

ALMOST A CINDERELLA STORY

Seattle protesters called Uber founder Travis Kalanick a sociopath, attempting, apparently, to insult him. He probably said "no shit" under his breath and laughed all the way to the bank. His methods are hardly new and not even close to being the most savage. These soft-headed protesters should check their rage at the door and take a history class if they want to understand what a real corporate shitshow is all about. Look at Travis's famous predecessor, steel titan Andrew Carnegie, whose incredibly profitable mills in Pittsburgh were so dangerously run that workers suffering "accidental death" there accounted, at one point, for 20 percent of all deaths of men in the city.[7] All Uber does is "routinely and aggressively sidestep the law and regulation; violate industry norms; ignore ethical boundaries; and trample on competitive relationships."[8] This is the perfect kind of place for you.

Now some may say it all caught up with Travis, turning his Uber into a pumpkin at midnight when he was forced to step down as chief executive. And sure, there is a certain dashing crash-and-burn quality to it: Uber's workplace culture has been exposed as condoning sexual harassment and discrimination,[9] and the company is under federal investigation for "greyballing," or using "a fake version of its app to evade law enforcement agencies."[10] Or you can think about it this way: federal inquiries often don't lead to criminal charges and greyballing helped Uber—now valued at $70 billion—break into markets in seventy countries. Travis is still worth about $7.1 billion.[11] He permanently disrupted the entire for-hire transportation business and now he doesn't even have to go to work.

The downside of some tech start-ups is all the "togetherness" and group think and brainstorming shit that goes down. You're not big into sharing. Also, everyone's so outrageously optimistic, firing off sanctimonious exhortations about changing the world *with an app* and posting vacuous shit like "live your truth" on the kitchen fridge. Easier said than done when you're supposed to clock in at least eighty hours a week and aren't considered "true blue" unless you sleep on a beanbag in a Silicon Valley romper room at least once a week. I mean, law firms require these kinds of hours from their new recruits too, but at least they let them go home and give them a driver. Plus, there are a few girls at a law firm. But all in all, if you can surf the chaos and stay away from the meetings, the tech start-up is a fantastic place for you.

Verdict: *Tech Start-up: Yes.*

Obviously, you know to avoid the few giant bureaucratic dinosaurs still around, filled with procedures, protocols, systems, and managers who will cramp your style and bore you to tears. But there's another kind of new company you should be equally wary of. Fans call them lifestyle companies. Those who find them creepy call them "nanny companies," or worse. They are often associated with maturing tech and have "campuses" instead of office buildings. Free lunch. "Bring your kids to work day" on Friday. Movie nights. Gardens and fountains. Loyalty perks like branded swag and passes to Disneyland. Velvety-voiced AI bots to help you when the network gets all fucked up. They want you to belong and to agree with them. Do it their way in a soporific daze stupefied by free lattes. Lots of people find this soothing and comfortable but it will drive you up the wall. It's really just a new form of control, run by a benevolent megalomaniac. They want to make you belong completely. To *them*. Without conflict. Compliant. This will not do.

You want what you want, not what they want. You don't give a shit about belonging and constant compliance is going to be exhausting. This place is far too cult-like for you. You'd rather start a dumpster fire.

Verdict: *Nanny Corp: No.*

WRITE A SELF-HELP BOOK

If you write a book that promises to help people get what they want because they want it, you could make a mint. Don't be shy, you don't have to be a great writer (you can always get a ghostwriter), you just need a good con.

In fact, a large majority of self-help books today simply regurgitate a few essential pioneers with some sort of personal expertise angle: I'm a diplomat (or a soldier, or a spy), and here's my take on how to get what you want based on what these other guys said. *Think and Grow Rich* by Napoleon Hill was an early seminal work. *How to Win Friends and Influence People* by Dale Carnegie is the gold standard. *Influence, the Power of Persuasion* by Robert Caldini was big for a while, and of course there is *The Secret*, an incredibly degraded yet

popular, latter-day version of the same crap whose vacuity was publicly supported by Oprah. Simple synopsis: Focus your mind on what you want and by "the law of attraction" you will get it. You and I know there is no such law and that the universe doesn't care about us. Doesn't "care" at all. But people love this kind of pap.

Verdict: *Write a Catchy Book that Promises People They Can Get What They Want Because They Want It: Yes.*

KEEP AN OPEN MIND

Don't be railroaded by the general population's perception that sociopaths are all either criminals, CEOs, or Wall Street stock traders. Don't get me wrong. These are excellent jobs for you if they fit with your natural talents, but stay open to other ideas. If you're more interested in controlling others than controlling money, consider becoming a preacher or starting a religion. If you are most interested in violence with impunity, look into police work, the secret service, or becoming a spy. According to Kevin Dutton's *The Wisdom of Psychopaths,* it's a little-known fact that sociopaths are overrepresented in many positions considered prosocial or "helping" positions like the ministry and civil service. (Because Dutton's test had to rely on volunteers, notably absent are famous people like politicians and entertainers. It's an imperfect list, but a promising start.) Here is his list of the UK's "most psychopathic professions":

1. CEO
2. Lawyer
3. Media TV/Radio Personality
4. Salesperson
5. Surgeon
6. Journalist
7. Police Officer
8. Clergyperson
9. Chef
10. Civil Servant[12]

Here are some possible reasons why these professions are included. (I'm skipping the more obvious ones.)

SURGEON; CHEF

If you are nimble, coordinated, and spatially aware, maybe slicing onions or eyeballs is just the ticket for you. Your cognitive strength is dorsal system mental processing. The dorsal system is the part of your brain concerned with "where" things are around you, not who they are or whether or not they're your friend. It guides your movements through space and uses logic and critical analysis (cold cognition), not emotion (hot cognition), to make decisions. It helps you stalk and track movement, and it works fast. Fallon describes your potential strength like this: "A psychopath has a poorly functioning ventral system, usually used for hot cognition, but can have a normal or even supernormal dorsal system, so that without the bother of conscience and empathy, the cold planning and execution of predatory behaviors becomes finely tuned, convincing, highly manipulative, and formidable."[13] That, plus a razor focus which makes you "very good at giving [your] undivided attention to things that interest [you] most and at ignoring other things"[14] could indeed make you well suited for the operating room or a high-end kitchen.

These strengths suggest you might also be a good hunter or ball player. Or that you also have OCD. But do note, if you do not have a hyperfunctioning dorsal system, your competing impulsiveness will wreak havoc on these kinds of jobs. Psychologist David Cox found that "soldiers who performed the exacting and dangerous task of defusing or dismantling IRA bombs referred to psychopaths as "cowboys"—unreliable and impulsive individuals who lacked the perfectionism and attention to detail needed to stay alive on the job."[15] So check your head before you sign up. Or stick with less lethal handiwork like a mechanic. If you know how to fix things, you will be respected and left alone.

Verdict: *Surgeon or Chef: Yes. Bomb Squad: Maybe.*

MEDIA PRODUCTION

> No one is likely to play an important part in the production of a feature film who is completely lacking in triadic skills.
>
> —Oliver James, *Office Politics*

The benefits of the entertainment industry for you are numerous. First, the arrangement is inherently chaotic and you will find it exciting. Every few months, a new coalition arises to facilitate a new project backed by a huge amount of money, involving volatile personalities, hundreds of moving parts, and no exact blueprint on how to proceed. Second, it runs on charm and personal magnetism, or star power. Third, project-based work with a defined end point can help those of you who lose focus and self-control after a while. You will have to deal with more sociopaths than in the average workplace, but blessed with a hard end date and the inevitable personnel shuffle, you should be able to move fast enough to stay ahead of trouble. The downside of project-based operations is you have to keep finding new work all the time. The key to this is keeping your act together until the very end. Word travels, and these businesses are smaller and more interconnected than you'd think.

Other production-based jobs provide the similar benefit of a good paycheck, a hard end date, and revolving personnel, like working a shift on an oil rig. But these jobs are more difficult and dangerous.

Verdict: *Media Production: Yes.*

CLERGY

Wait, did somebody just say Jim Jones? While many see the ministry as a good, selfless, and helpful profession, it also provides three things that are extremely attractive to you: cover, influence, and an attentive crowd whose minds are dominated by belief rather than critical thinking.

RELIGIOUS GREATS

If you want to extend your reach as a religious visionary (warning: this can get you killed), you must think big. The more spectacular and outlandish the claim, the better the results will be.

Jesus convinced people he was the son of God. He was so good at it, that this belief has persisted for thousands of years, convincing hundreds of millions of people and causing countless wars. The downside: Jesus was crucified.

Joseph Smith, the father of the Mormon religion, claimed to have dug up some holy gold tablets that were conveniently located on his farm.

He *lost* these priceless artifacts but recreated what they said by staring into a hat. Along with pronouncements by an angel named Moroni and a decree that you shouldn't drink coffee, Smith preached that Jesus came to America and hung out with the American Indians. Mormonism has spanned the globe and in the 1980s and 1990s was the fastest growing religion on planet earth. Downside: Smith was lynched.

L. Ron Hubbard, founder of Scientology, spent a great deal of time and effort to get his teachings classified as a religion rather than a form of quack self-help psychology (he hated psychologists) because, as a religion, you get tax-exempt status—another plus in the religion business.

Hubbard convinced millions that a foreign race of aliens called Thetans were dumped into prehistoric volcanoes, and their spirits now inhabit us, creating negative energy you can only get rid of by paying the "church" outrageous sums of money. If this sounds batshit crazy, it's because it is. But it sure makes a lot of money. Downside: Hubbard spent the latter part of his life in hiding from the IRS and died under mysterious circumstances.

I recently received a Dianetics questionnaire in the mail which is brilliantly constructed so that no matter how you answer, your score indicates that you are in dire need of Scientology. It's a closed loop. No matter what you answer, you need Scientology. If you can trap people like this, you are one step ahead. Successful cults are really good not only at offering a secret promise—if you come inside, we will tell you the thing you desperately want to know, the thing which will rid you of the pain of being a human being—but are also great at getting you to invest yourself and increasingly believe you need to follow them so that by the time the secret is revealed to you as it must be, an empty box, you are already brainwashed. Ex–Scientology member Jason Beghe describes the church's methods excellently. "If I'm trying to enslave somebody . . . the best trap is you get a guy to just keep himself in jail. And that's what scientology does. You just keep yourself in jail. . . . You believe it and you're investing your time and your money and so . . . you can't be a fool. That's too much to confront."[16] Scientology also employs an effective defense maneuver you should try when under pressure. They call it "Fair Game" which is shorthand for never defend, always attack. It has worked well for them. Use it.

Another influential 1950s religious player sometimes known as "God's salesman" was Pastor Norman Vincent Peale. He straddled the religion/self-help line with his book *The Power of Positive Thinking* where he promoted unmitigated self-confidence, saying "formulate and staple indelibly on your mind a mental picture of yourself as succeeding. Hold this picture tenaciously. Never permit it to fade." He also promoted the idea that somehow belief in the gospel can be used to unleash material success. (By the way, this dude was Donald Trump's pastor as a child.) From this seed, the whole aspirational religious movement known as "Prosperity Gospel" has sprouted televangelists and megachurches all over the country, funded by the idea that God will give you money and health if you prove you are a good follower by giving lots of money to your church. If you can convince people of this, you could well have your own gilded megachurch in a strip mall one day.

Verdict: *Clergy: Yes. But you might get killed.*

We could go on like this for days, but you get the idea. Identify your best sociopathic traits, steer toward them and away from your least controllable urges. Impulsive? Predator? Disagreeable? Go through the different sociopathic professions discussed and play to your strengths. Hone in on a field of expertise where you'll be best suited to crush and win while at the same time appearing confident, valuable, and promotable.

EMPLOYMENT TESTS

Between your resume and the interview seat lies some kind of gatekeeper whose main task is to assess whether or not you are technically qualified *and* whether or not your psychological temperament, look, and character are suitable for the job and the company "culture." You may be tempted to brush these people off as petty and irrelevant but *do not underestimate them.* One of their favorite tools is the personality test. While it's unlikely HR is going to give you the Hare psychopathy test, their questions will echo certain concerns about what is surely lurking inside you. In 2013, 57 percent of large US employers used pre-hire assessments[17] to screen applicants before the interview phase. These can be hacked. They can be beaten. But not in exactly the way you might think. Before you take any test, you should familiarize yourself with the way they work.

First, know that when they tell you "There are no right or wrong answers," they are lying. Of course there are.

In 1956, William Whyte published a book called *The Organization Man* which looked into the rise of the Human Relations department and their unbridled enthusiasm for "scientism." The idea being that a person's mind, self, what have you, could one day be profiled and described with scientific exactitude. You would become a psychological certainty as identifiable as a cancer cell or a string of genes. When the research was finally completed, who "you" are would have an answer. An answer that would provide an accurate and proven prognosticator of a valuable and successful employee.

HR: "Here's Bill, he's a forty-six."
Manager: "Great, set him up in the hive. All forty-sixes thrive on big data. Put him by the window."
HR: "What else do you need?"
Manager: "I've got some real dog shit to clean up. I need a forty-one, a nine-nine-six, and a Blue Ox."

The scientism folks wanted to eliminate conflict, promote worker peace and stability, and get everyone to buy a Weber grill and move to the suburbs. Obviously that never happened. Seventy years later, personality tests have been refined, but are fundamentally the same.

Many companies judge you based on how similar your test results are to those of their current employees. "We use our existing employees that we know are really good at the job and then try to find people who [test] just like them," said John Marick, cofounder of Consumer Cellular, a cell phone service company.[18] This means they compare your results against those of people who already work there. If you match, you get the job. If not, adios. Well, that's a trying little closed loop: if a person can't get into the company in the first place because he doesn't match the type of people who already work there, he can't very well serve as a successful model for new prospects. Deal with it, that's the way it works. They don't want to know how great or brilliant or unique you are, just how close you come to being like their existing successful employees. Taking a moment to read up on the company mission statements and press releases can help you get into the mind-set of what their ideal employee might be like; craft your answers accordingly.

Much of Whyte's advice on how to cheat on personality tests[19] still works. Because, as a sociopath, you tend to really emphasize how great you are, pay attention to this piece of Whyte's advice: "You don't win a good score: you avoid a bad one. . . . Your safety lies in getting a score somewhere between the 40th and 60th percentiles, which is to say, you should try to answer as if you were like everybody else is supposed to be. . . . When asked for word associations or comments about the world, give the most conventional, run-of-the-mill, pedestrian answer possible."

And as far as eliminating any "bad" characteristics, don't overdo it. Whyte continues "these tests almost always have lie scores built into them." This means a too-perfect score will indicate you are lying." A few mild neuroses conceded here and there won't give you too bad a score, and in conceding neuroses you should know that more often than not you have the best margin for error if you err on the side of being "hypermanic"—that is, too energetic and active. Don't be too dominant."[20] Remember, these tests are all about psychological profiling and often contain nothing related to the specific tasks the job requires. Your core personality is being probed and you have a secret to keep.

Some other pieces of advice:

- Be psychologically consistent with your answers. (Don't say you're super-imaginative and also super-conscientious because they both seemed like the "right" answer at the time. Actually, don't say you're super-anything.)
- When in doubt, always say you like people.
- Avoid condescending statements.
- Don't overthink the answers. If you get too clever or cute, you will come off as being duplicitous. Many online tests even have a timer recording how long you take to answer each question. A slow response time gives the impression you are "overthinking," a.k.a. "trying to figure out what they want to hear," a.k.a. "lying." This can negatively affect your score.

–   Don't get paranoid. Remember, the HR people are *not* there to out
you as a sociopath. They are not the police. They just want to know
if you are a fit. If anything, their radar is more targeted toward
keeping out a loud misfit than a Ted Bundy from their exclusive
and wonderful office culture. (Remember, they once had to take
this test and were deemed A-OK, and they feel proud of this.) Stay
relaxed and moderate.

Many tests are based on the Big Five personality traits, known by the cute
anagram "OCEAN." These five overarching personality traits are perceived to
define a person's broad characteristics and, by extension, job suitability. You
want to rate high-ish on the positive traits and low-ish on the negative.

Positive traits:
Openness. Imaginative, expansive, interested in new things.
Conscientiousness. Reliable, organized, thorough.
Extroversion. Energetic, assertive.
Agreeableness. Cooperative, friendly, compassionate.
Negative trait:
Neuroticism. Emotionally unstable, negative emotions.

Low agreeableness is the most important red flag for a sociopath like
you to avoid triggering. On personality tests, you tend to score significantly
lower than average on agreeability ratings. According to psychologist Dan P.
McAdams, "People low in agreeableness are described as callous, rude, arrogant,
and lacking in empathy. . . . [They] are typically viewed as untrustworthy."[21]
People want you to behave, and have for decades. Here's a sample principle
from General Electric's "Effective Presentation" course from 1956: "Never say
anything controversial."[22] This course also claimed, "You can always get anybody to do what you wish"—a sentiment we wholeheartedly agree with. This
advice to act inoffensively will help you on these tests, but it's also a good idea
in general. Act agreeable as often as possible. This does not mean be spineless,
weak, or ready to capitulate. It doesn't mean be a timid pushover in pleated
chinos. It just means don't bite someone's fucking head off for not setting up
the cloud password on your keychain. Go about your business and do what

you need to do, just keep the unnecessary caustic remarks or bitchiness to a minimum.

It will take a little work on your part to get a good score on "conscientiousness," as you'll have to cover up for the fact that you naturally possess exactly none. But don't overdo it, this is all about getting past HR and getting a job you are going to have to deal with, possibly for years, so don't lie about everything. Just the disagreeableness thing.

Oh and careful with the neurotic thing. McAdams continues, "Higher scores on neuroticism are always bad, having proved to be a risk factor for unhappiness, dysfunctional relationships, and mental-health problems."[23]

If you want to practice, and analyze your scores, take an OCEAN test online—one place you can do it is at https://ocean.cambridgeanalytica.org/— to see how you score. (Yes, these kind of sites are likely analyzing and selling your data.)

Idea #1: Before you take the test for the job you really want, try taking a few "practice" tests by applying for jobs you have no interest in, but have online questionnaires. Pick five at random. Answer the first questionnaire truthfully. Your lack of interest will help prevent you from protecting yourself. For the others, read up on the job, the company "creed," and any company newsletters or employee bios you can find to get a flavor for who they consider themselves to be. Take the other tests, combining the above-mentioned tips with the company's advertised values, and try to play an ideal employee. See which interviews you get. Study your performance. Tell them you already have a job, but thanks for the offer. When your test to call-back ratio improves, you are ready to move on to the real company you are interested in. (Note that the first company is not calling you back.) Keep in mind, the questions and answers will not remain static. You are engaged in a game of psychic cat and mouse. Know that as you hack the tests, the test designers are also learning how to hide the "correct" response from you.

Idea #2: If you are actually skilled at what you do, try to find companies that are testing for aptitude rather than personality. Aptitude tests are less psychologically tricky, tend to be more factually accurate, and can show off your skills without exposing your dark side.

Many companies also employ criminal record and credit checks which are cheaper and easier to run online than ever before. Not having an arrest record is obviously preferred. But if you do have one, it's worth paying a lawyer to get convictions reduced from felonies to misdemeanors when allowable by law (which is more often than you'd think) and make sure any arrests that didn't result in a conviction are properly expunged, otherwise they're probably still lurking in your digital skeleton closet. If you do get confronted with your arrest record by some nosy prying gatekeeper, act embarrassed, but then gently remind her that the FBI currently has 77.7 *million* people on file for arrest, which is almost *one in three of all adults* in the USA.[24] Tell her you were just in the wrong place at the wrong time, or the cops told you the breathalyzer was faulty, but they needed to meet their quota. If that doesn't work, try telling a joke or changing the subject.

CHAPTER 4

ACING THE INTERVIEW

Do you swear to tell the truth, the whole truth and nothing but the truth?
Don't make me laugh.

—John Banville, *The Book of Evidence*

You've outsmarted the personality tests and gotten through the HR force
field, but don't get cocky. This just means they think you're mentally
acceptable for the job. You shook the psychological eight ball and used your
tilt skills to surface that "Signs point to yes" message . . . but this just means
your real charm work is about to begin. Luckily, you know you're going to be
scrutinized in the job interview, so you can prepare. Yes, you naturally make a
good first impression, and that's great, but don't get lazy and rely on it. In the
interview, you need to give off not just a good impression, but the impression
that you are talented yet humble and a team player, well suited for the job,
highly motivated, and in demand. Getting things right straight out of the gate
will make things insanely easier for you, so this is the time to strike.

"You don't get a second chance to make a first impression"[1] is common
knowledge, but why? In *Blink*, Malcolm Gladwell suggests people are extremely
good at rapid cognition or what he calls "thin-slicing" which is the ability to
pick up a huge amount of complex situational information in an incredibly
short period of time. He says:

A person watching a silent two-second video clip of a teacher he or she
has never met will reach conclusions about how good that teacher is that

are very similar to those of a student who has sat in the teacher's class for an entire semester. That's the power of our adaptive unconscious.

The moment you walk into the room, the interviewer is thin-slicing you whether he's aware of it or not. He's never met you before. He knows what he decides about you could have a serious effect on his own future and well-being. He's paying close attention to you, actively interpreting the minutest cues you display in order to make a decision about who you are as quickly as possible. His job may well depend on it. The interviewer is using automatic thinking rather than rational thinking. What behavioral theorists Thaler and Sunstein call the "Automatic System" of decision making "is rapid and . . . instinctive, and it does not involve what we usually associate with the word *thinking*."[2] It relies heavily on bias to create belief about who you are. Based on the above evidence, it seems we are very good at collecting an accurate impression quickly and on first meeting.

But perhaps this consistency between first impression and lasting impression only happens when the person creating the impression does so unconsciously and in earnest. Because in direct opposition to these findings, psychologist Amy Cuddy confirms that social psychology "has amassed a great deal of evidence that humans persistently make biased decisions based on minimal, misleading, and misunderstood first impressions. We've clearly demonstrated that first impressions are often flimsy and dangerous."[3] This suggests that with a little preparation, attention to detail, and a few tools, you can control those same judgments, creating a first impression that works for you, rather than represents who you "really" are. This chapter will help you understand what cues the interviewer is looking for, what common beliefs influence him, and, therefore, what positive impressions you can foster without even lying. However you engineer your first impression it's important to remember the interviewer is highly attentive and suggestible, and the results will be persistent.

EXPRESSIVE COHERENCE

The most important thing you can do in an interview is something the interviewer probably doesn't even realize he's looking for. It's not that you must be qualified or charming. It's a purely negative baseline need: *you must not appear to be sketchy or full of shit in any way.* Your "presentation of self" must be without contradiction.

According to social psychologist Erving Goffman, you provide two kinds of information in any interaction. The first is what the other person presumes you control consciously (what you are saying). The second, he presumes you are not conscious of and therefore not actively manipulating (nonverbal gestures, your "vibe," etc.). When your conscious and unconscious cues harmonize, the interviewer will relax and believe you really are who you say you are. This is what Goffman calls EXPRESSIVE COHERENCE.[4] Some people call it the sigh of relief.

Conversely, clashing messages between the conscious and unconscious cues (saying "I'd love to" while making a fist) creates an awful, alarming dissonance that taps into some primal survival instinct. Get out of here! Something's not right! An instinct that caused your ancestors to leap shrieking across the veldt away from a deadly rising leopard, who moments ago appeared to be mere dapples in a shady tree. It is the fairy tale fear of wolves dressed as kindly grandmothers and sheep.

When you fail to project expressive coherence, it's like what actors call breaking character; the illusion you are presenting as your "self" falls apart. This is very distressing to the person you are presenting to, because they're suddenly forced to deal with two contradictory realities concerning you: who you are presenting and what's really going on beneath the surface. This causes COGNITIVE DISSONANCE, a psychological discomfort that comes about whenever two conflicting beliefs present themselves. The moment the other person catches a whiff of dissonance, they'll distrust you, and the interview is over. Humans are very sensitive to cognitive dissonance and you don't have to be actively lying for them to know something is amiss. They'll grow instantly wary and uneasy when they sense you are not who you present yourself to be. The effect is strong and must be avoided, no matter what. As you are a wolf yourself, mind your cues carefully.

You can learn to recognize and control this unconscious information to create a positive, seamless impression. Lots of self-help books—stealing from Dale Carnegie—suggest you have a "firm handshake" and "crinkle your eyes when you smile" to seem genuine instead of forced. This is excellent, time-tested advice. Some even go as far as to suggest you put numbing cream on your lips to keep them from twitching when you're nervous but want to seem relaxed,[5] but this is just goofy.

Goffman described presenting with expressive coherence as knowing how to "protect your own projections." Your best approach is to avoid setting off cognitive dissonance in others in the first place. Foster the impression you have an expressively coherent self and keep contradictory ideas from colliding out in the open as much as possible

EXPLOITING COGNITIVE DISSONANCE

Beyond a failure of expressive coherence, cognitive dissonance more broadly defines the mental discomfort caused by two conflicting beliefs—a psychological paradox. These vex people. People find them irritating, and because they don't want to wonder or worry, they will choose one of the incongruent traits to define who the person really is and discard the rest.

In George Orwell's *1984,* DOUBLETHINK is a brainwashing technique that gives people "the power of holding two contradictory beliefs in one's mind simultaneously, and accepting both of them."[6] In fact, the population in 1984 is so beyond feeling mental distress at contradiction, they happily accept the impossible veracity of oxymoronic state slogans like "War is Peace" or "Freedom is Slavery." But this is science fiction, and most people find it exhausting to live with conflicting beliefs, with people who don't make sense, with constant cognitive dissonance. If you want to be in control, learn to embrace the unresolved, live with contradictions, and leave things ambiguous and undecided. This will irritate the people around you to the point where they'll do just about anything to make you make sense.

For example, if you want to destabilize that jerk Justin in accounting, a little cognitive dissonance can work wonders. Throw out some competing "facts" that don't fit together. You know Justin thinks VP Bruce is a genius, top-of-the-line. Look at the numbers Justin presents and say "I can't believe it. If these numbers really are correct, Bruce's plan will go completely off the rails by Q4." Justin is suddenly faced with a crisis: either his belief that Bruce is a genius is false or his own accounting is mistaken. Justin will backtrack, he might even melt his own mind from the inside with doubt. You've thrown him for a minute. It's sadly easy to do.

More fun though, is next-level dissonance control. Say, you want to fuck with Dan, who is probably about to get promoted instead of you. You start the same way: go to Justin and say, "If these numbers really are correct, Bruce's plan is completely batshit." Okay so you've introduced dissonance in Justin, but how to make it work for you? Offer him a new solution—"Are you sure these aren't Dan's numbers?" Back this up with some proof that some of these numbers did indeed seem to come from Dan—through a carelessly worded email taken out of context, for example. You have now offered Dan's incompetence as the cure for Justin's dissonance. You can salt the pot with some additional discordant sweet nothings, if you want—"If Dan really believed this plan was going to work, would he still be driving that car?"—but what you've now got is an ally (Justin) who will do whatever he can to take down Dan in order to preserve his own piece of mind. Dissonance is amazing stuff.

Develop your naturally high tolerance for dissonance. Open endings. Ambiguity. Leave your shoes untied. You can literally drive people crazy this way. They will keep trying to "fix it" or "settle" it. Just keep kicking the can down the road and these people will keep struggling valiantly to "solve" the problem. Eventually when they come up with an answer that's useful to you, then you can agree with them.

> When . . . *The Wild Bunch* premiered, a woman journalist raised her hand at the press conference and asked the following: "Why in the world do you have to show so much blood all over the place?" . . . Ernest Borgnine, looked a bit perplexed and fielded the question. "Lady, did you ever see anyone shot by a gun without bleeding?" . . . That's gotta be one of the principles behind reality. Accepting things that are hard to comprehend, and leaving them that way. And bleeding. Shooting and bleeding.
>
> —Haruki Murakami, *Sputnik Sweetheart*

DISSONANCE DAMAGE CONTROL

DOUBLESPEAK as opposed to doublethink, is a real-world solution to tamping down cognitive dissonance by using tricky language to obscure the conflict between competing realities. Euphemisms are effective for this kind of work. In a country where a majority believe themselves to be good Christians who love their fellow man, why say "torture" when you can say "enhanced interrogation," or "civilian casualty" when you've got "collateral damage." Long the playground of politicians smoothing over unpleasant things in far-away places, these velvet words are intended to make people feel more comfortable with something profoundly jarring and at odds with their idea of themselves. The British are really good at this stuff. For example, when someone visibly hammered makes it into tabloids, they are commonly described as "tired and emotional" instead of "drunk."[7] This method pretty well stinks and people are wise to it. It's more fun and effective to call out someone else's feeble attempt to hide behind euphemisms. If a coworker tries to say he was tired and emotional, you can respond, "I don't disagree with you, Stanley, but you did puke all over the elevator." The laugh you get will destroy the euphemism's power.

Keep in mind that jokes are a good way to make light of disruptions in your expressive coherence. They remove a sense of seriousness and can relieve tension. If someone makes a joke at your expense, ask them to explain it. Jokes lose vitality when they have to be explained.

SPIN is another popular method for patching up a bad situation by reducing cognitive dissonance. Rather than employing euphemisms to dampen the news itself, spin concentrates on framing it in a way to seem less shocking. One method is to compare the breaking news with similar underreported realities. The news: "Brand X kills baby rabbits!" The dissonance: "Oh no, but I love brand X, it keeps my lawn so green!" The spin: "Despite the recent baby rabbit tragedy at Hotel Lapin, there is no evidence Brand X poses a greater threat to baby rabbits than any other lawn fertilizer." Cognitive relief: "Phew, Brand X isn't really to blame. I can keep using it, just like I want to." Other forms of spin include cherry-picking choice quotations and both surpressing and leaking significant details. ALTERNATIVE FACTS are a form of spin which will hopefully be left discarded as a footnote to 2017 politics; file under bullshit.

No matter the method, cognitive dissonance is a powerful force people will go to great lengths to alleviate. In *Catch 22,* Joseph Heller describes the resulting distortion of belief as a *protective rationalization*:

The chaplain had mastered, in a moment of divine intuition, the handy technique of protective rationalization, and he was exhilarated by his discovery. It was miraculous. It was almost no trick at all, he saw, to turn vice into virtue and slander into truth, impotence into abstinence, arrogance into humility, plunder into philanthropy, thievery into honor, blasphemy into wisdom, brutality into patriotism, and sadism into justice. Anybody could do it; it required no brains at all. It merely required no character.[8]

You are perfectly suited for this.

The following sections illuminate some of the unconscious cues people are always reading beyond the smile crinkles around your eyes. As you look at them keep this principal of coherence in mind. Ask yourself, *Who am I saying I am?* And, *How can I present this same thing with my body, my clothes, or my voice?* If you can keep your unconscious gestures and your conscious assertions in line with one another, if you can express coherence, nothing will get in your way.

Practice your expressive coherence. In the limited setting of the interview, you can have far more control over your unconscious gestures than most people would believe. Practice your gestures, your posture. Watch *Sex, Lies, and Videotape* a few times to familiarize yourself with the raw extreme of what interviews can reveal. Then relax. You totally won't have to deal with questions even remotely as touchy as the ones in that movie. Record yourself answering practice questions while speaking directly to the camera. Watch the result, keeping an eye out for any creepiness you might display, like excessive eye contact (some eye contact is good, staring is not). If you can't tell yourself, get someone to watch the tape and see how they react. Do they cringe when you laugh? Do not to take it out on the watcher! Work on it. The watcher shouldn't be your mom. In fact, the less they know you the better. Hire a task rabbit to do it. Say it is an audition tape and ask them to describe the character you're playing. If they say "a sociopath" you're back at square one. Then try it again. Keep practicing until the tape reveals a calm, confident, trustworthy person.

> ### TRUE CONFESSIONS
>
> "I would describe myself as someone who is clear headed, alert, attuned. I see things for what they are without needing to swaddle them in comforting fictions. Sociopaths don't blink as often as other people do, which makes others think us lizard-like and cold, but it's just that we don't share the same need to look away from reality. A blink is a tiny blindness, a momentary hiding, a dark private space in which to cower and coddle your fear. We are not afraid and only blink when we need to moisten our eyes."
>
> —Daniel Smith, Falconer. Cooke City, Montana.

BODY LANGUAGE

The science is in. Embodied cognition is real. How we hold ourselves affects how we perceive ourselves, and how others perceive us. The evidence is persuasive that certain postures build confidence, and most importantly, allow us to steamroll people.

"Expansive, open body language is closely tied to dominance. . . . When we feel powerful, we make ourselves bigger,"[9] says psychologist Amy Cuddy. She cites research showing cortisol (stress) and testosterone (aggression) levels change in the body based on posture, and promotes her body-control tips as a way to help sad, anxious people who feel like an impostor or a fraud be empowered. You're an impostor, you're just not anxious. Her big finding is that practicing a "power posture" *before* you walk into a room is what makes it effective.

If you want to brush up on your Power Stance, watch her Ted talk.[10] Just be warned, she will probably irritate the living shit out of you. She's basically saying all you have to do is go into a bathroom stall and stand like Wonder Woman for two minutes and you can become powerful and able to get what you want. It's easy and effective. But whatever you do, don't let anyone see you. Her *Ted Talk* has had millions of views, so if anyone who's seen it glimpses you in a Wonder Woman pose, they will assume you are insecure and suffering from shitty self-esteem, which in turn will empower them to come after you. If you need to "power up" someplace where you might get seen, consider doing a "Nixon" instead.

The paranoid and brilliant Richard Nixon tried his hand at embodied cognition after losing to young upstart John F. Kennedy. During their televised debate, Nixon looked sweaty and shifty, while handsome Kennedy stared straight into the camera with a good haircut and the world's toothiest smile. This really pissed Nixon off. According to Cuddy's references, Tricky Dick's "Double V for Victory" posture should have an empowering effect, and if someone catches you doing it, they might think you're crazy, but never a sucker.

Nixon missed one key part in this finding: It's a *pre-posture* . . . if you do it at showtime, it doesn't work *at all*.

Tip: If you are forced into a corner where you feel you are being perceived as too aggressive, flip the script. Ask why *they* are using dominant body language and ask curiously, as if you are genuinely interested, without anger or fear. If they perceive you as hostile, you risk elevating the stakes into a macho standoff.

MIRRORING. Echoing the body language of your interviewer is an effective way to make them see you as desirable and acceptable because they feel you are like them[11] and will be comfortable around you. They stroke the chin, you stroke the chin. They adjust their balls and recross their legs, you mirror. Ad infinitum. Every gesture you make which they see as a reflection (or "similar to") themselves will make them feel more relaxed around you. And the funny thing is they won't even notice it. Mirroring is a natural, friendly reaction, a soothing gesture of goodwill placing a warm, fuzzy, hypnotic "no need to worry about this guy" blanket over the interviewer's lazy brain. (For a great example of mirroring, look at this clip of Tom Waits and Australian host Don Lane during a 1979 interview: https://www.youtube.com/watch?v=tsRbhBXPgKk.)

An expression of empathy and rapport, mirroring is not exactly natural for you, and if it's not done right, the unnaturalness of your movements will cause alarm. You might be perceived as autistic or ill or nervous, so take your time. Work on it slowly. If your interviewer frowns, don't jerk your face into a tragic rictus, just droop your lips a little. If the interviewer crosses his leg at the knee, cross yours a moment later at the ankle. It should be a fluid conversation of movements, not as the name implies, a literal mirror.

PERVERSE REVERSE. Not suitable for an interview situation, but once you have the job and have some control, one effective way of putting someone off is to avoid mirroring them. While people don't usually notice mirroring because it puts them at ease, they will notice non-mirroring and take it as an expression of hostility. They'll become uncomfortable, but won't know exactly why. Here's a conversation that will never take place:

> Diane: "I think Max feels hostile toward me."
> Jake: "Why?"
> Diane: "He didn't cross his arms when I did."
> Jake: "Oh yeah, you were out of synchrony. You're in for it now."

CODE SWITCHING

> When rich people do something nice for you, you give 'em a pot of jam.
> —John Guare, *Six Degrees of Separation*

The phrase *code switching* sounds official yet secretive and mysterious, and is a nice way to think about managing your first impression. I am appropriating it. Originally, it was a linguistic term used to signify how people change the way they speak in order to fit in with those around them. Presidential nominee Obama said "Nah, we straight"[12] when the cashier asked if he wanted his change at Ben's Chili Bowl in a black Washington, DC, neighborhood, but he certainly wouldn't have said the same to Putin. But code switching can also effectively describe the ways we contrive to broadcast "this is who I am" or "I'm in your club" cues to others with our manner and appearance. These cues are very specific to time and place. In the nineteenth century, it was stylish for German aristocrats to *cut their own faces* to create what looked like dueling scars in order to transmit an aura of bravery and status. But today, mutilated faces are considered a sign of suicidal tendencies. From class rings to pinky rings, sideburns to tasseled loafers, the physical details you present will be presumed to say a lot about you; use them to present yourself as someone who belongs.

How is this special for the sociopath? For most people, code switching is a concerted effort to broadcast who you "are" in order to attract like-minded people. But you don't want to attract like people. You want to stay away from like people. And you don't want to broadcast who you really "are" at all. At the same time, you don't want to appear too bland and featureless. You don't want to just show up in the appropriately priced, brand-approved suit for the job (though you should take care to study and *know* what that would be) because this will make you seem either really boring, or make people suspect you are hiding something. You want to betray a few details that give the impression that you have an interesting and meaningful private life. You want to *seem* like you are trying to attract successful, thoughtful, interesting people such as yourself. But you also don't want to come off as trying too hard. Pick a few of the following to concentrate on.

CLOTHES

> Clean as a broke dick dog.
> —Miles Davis, describing a sharp dresser

Haircuts, shoes, glasses, watches, phones, even perfumes are a quick indicator of your social group, place of origin, income status, and level of meticulousness. You will be judged instantly based on these things. Even things like tiny scars from the earrings-a-guy-wore-in-high-school are noticed and taken into account. The first level of dressing is, of course, meant to show respect for the position you are seeking. Clean, polished, suave, honest, appropriate, etc. It's actually funny how simple some dressing errors are that make people think you're desperately broke or totally insane: Unzipped fly. Mismatching shoes or socks. A noticeable run in your stockings, especially above the knee. Stains of any kind, especially under the armpit. Chipped glasses. Don't wear these things. Ever. It's better to go in underdressed and clean. You should know this by now. But there's more.

> I have found that people believe that a man in a bowtie will steal.
> —John T. Molloy, *Dress for Success*

It's not just about getting one over on your interviewer by displaying the cues he wants to see, studies now show your own brain function is affected by what you wear. Like embodied cognition, ENCLOTHED COGNITION is real. "Clothing you wear affects your psychological processes. . . . Your outfit alter[s] how you approach and interact with the world."[13] In a study by Adam D. Galinsky, subjects who wore a "doctor's coat" showed more "sustained and heightened attention" compared to those who wore the identical coat, but were told it was a "painter's coat."[14] So dress smart for yourself.

You need to employ a next-level of code switching in order to subtly influence your interviewer. Back in the day, people used to wear class rings to indicate their alma mater; it was an instant indicator that you are in the club. Now, people wear tiny shiny flag pins on their lapels to signify patriotism. But these are still too general. You want to subtly express something to your interviewer which links you specifically to him. While this can be tricky to pull off without being obvious, it can be done to great effect. This requires you learn a little bit about him. Personality will affect your potential boss's sense of style.

> I have two rules. One is, never trust a man who smokes a pipe. The other is, never trust a man with shiny shoes.
>
> —Charles Bukowski, *Hollywood*

Get to know the reputation of your potential boss. Flashy? Show some class with a Rolex, even if it's a twenty-buck knockoff from Canal Street. He likely won't notice it's a fake, but if he does, admire his sharp eyesight, admit it's not real, and tell him you aspire to own the genuine article someday.

A certain successful headhunter in New York City, whom we'll call Caroline, wears a strange-looking black stone necklace to challenging interviews. When clients ask her what it is—which they invariably do—she tells them it was made from her mother's ashes. (Her mother is alive and well). This instantly catches the client off guard, knocks them back, and makes them feel Caroline has revealed something very private and sensitive, thereby softening them up and allowing her to probe into their unguarded secret selves.

PROPS

For technical jobs, showing up with the right gadgets and proper, high-quality (but not new) tools of the trade are important to show you are an expert. While a few key active props are great, you're not a juggler, so don't get too cute with the show-and-tell. And remember, you can also use latent props that you and your interviewer will both pretend not to pay attention to: a Tiffany bag set down casually by the door, for instance, says you are a classy, thoughtful guy with a hot wife or mistress.

> The bag is a valuable prop in this kind of work; mine has a lot of baggage tags on it—SF, LA, NY, Lima, Rome, Bangkok, that sort of thing—and the most prominent tag of all is a very official, plastic-coated thing that says "Photog. Playboy Mag." I bought it from a pimp in Vail, Colorado, and he told me how to use it. "Never mention *Playboy* until you're sure they've seen this thing first," he said. "Then, when you see them notice

it, that's the time to strike. They'll go belly-up every time. This thing is magic, I tell you. Pure magic.

—Hunter S. Thompson,
"The Kentucky Derby is Decadent and Depraved"

Props can also be used effectively once you've passed the interview stage and are moving into your new office. It's important to mind the little things. Even in the most monotonous cubicle-filled office, almost everyone will have something personal at their desk. And so should you, because everyone will notice what your thing is, and judge you by it. A totally barren desk will make you seem conspicuously dull. The safest thing is a picture of your spouse and kids or your dog. A droll mug is acceptable, an alma-mater mug makes you seem pretentious. Because there is so little of your personal life in evidence, people will make more of these desktop items than they should. When in doubt, opt for funny. Try something goofy and mildly risqué like one of those pens containing a mermaid whose bikini top disappears when you flip the thing upside down.

WHITEY'S RAT

Don't give yourself away with the wrong kind of personal props. Items from Whitey Bulger's estate were recently auctioned off for over one hundred thousand dollars. Aside from a few items that actually had intrinsic value (gold, diamonds, etc.) the most coveted objects were those thought to express his pitch-black personality. Two of the most fiercely bidded-for items (sometimes known as murderabilia) were a silver skull ring and a pencil holder carved in the shape of a rat, signifying Whitey's extreme hatred of snitches. This type of juvenile shit instantly nails you as a psychopath. Don't bring it to work.

PROTECT YOUR SOURCES

A famous author I know wraps her *Idiot's Guide to . . . Whatever* books on her office shelf in brown paper, like old-school textbooks, so no one who comes in can see she's consulted anything but the most highbrow, original, and difficult-to-read source material. She comes off as awfully clever.

The eighties book *Power!* offers this tip, I think in all sincerity. While crazy and dated, it would be funny as an *SNL* sketch: "A nice touch is to leave out two or three red folders marked 'Confidential' and to push them out of sight once any visitor has noticed them."[15] Just make sure they're bright flaming red. Because everybody keeps their confidential shit in bright flaming red folders marked "Confidential" on their desk.

MANNERS

Manners are largely used by men of the world as a means of self-concealment.

—Edward Alsworth Ross, *Social Control*

Almost every movie about an uptight rich family vetting their child's prospective mate has some scene where manners rule the day: Can Johnny properly dismember a lobster? Can Julia pluck a roasted snail from its shell without accidentally flinging it across the restaurant? Who cares? They do. And because they have the money, they get to. It's the same way neat freaks have the right to berate slobs but not vice versa, even when the slob might be a genius visual thinker, and the one who makes his bed every morning with hospital corners is a useless hysteric germaphobe. If you slurp your soup, you are an unworthy boor. You may think this is dumb and you are free to rail against the judgment of Aunt Sue by drinking the dressing from your salad bowl. But an interview or lunch meeting is a different affair. It's not about asserting your rights, it's about making the others comfortable enough with your habits to relax their scrutiny of your true self.

Don't be intimidated by manners. Remember, (if you believe the scientists,) man has been around in some form for roughly six million years, civilization for roughly six thousand years. And forks were considered weird and sinister as late as the early eighteenth century when Louis XIV himself would not allow his own children to eat with them.[16] People act like "it has always been thus." No, it hasn't. Many social niceties are acts of aggression. Shaking hands was originally intended to prove you're not carrying a weapon. Standing at the table when a guest approached allowed you to unsheathe your sword if necessary.[17] What's the point of this for you? Learn manners and use them. They're not some mystical age-old secret held by those with "class." People make them out to be more difficult or exclusive than they are. Employing impeccable manners will help you hide. That said, if you are at a lunch meeting, don't order a lobster.

ACCENTS

> Y'all sound like the *news*.
>
> —U. Oregon freshman from Tennessee

Are people going to judge you based you on your accent? Yes. There are countless studies that show if you sound Mexican or African American—or have a minority-sounding name—you will have a harder time getting an interview.[18] If you sound regional, people assume you're uneducated, unworldly, or dumb. Sounding foreign may give you an exotic flair but people will judge you based on the country's stereotype. Sounding French or British may help you. Sounding Russian, not so much. Terrible, but true.

Perhaps you have one of these accents. What should you do about it? First off, whenever possible, present yourself in person and avoid the phone. When someone sees you, they'll be dazzled by all the positive cues you're giving off and your accent will become relatively less important. Lots of people go to speech therapists to get rid of an accent. But, suppose you fake your accent and get the job. You're going to have to sound like that until you quit or get fired, which is going to be a drag.

Maybe there's another way. Eleven percent of Londoners admit to adapting a less posh accent so they sound more working-class and less like a ponce when trying to get a job or a date.[19] Probably because the Beatles or Keith Richards or whoever made this cool. Concentrate on your vocabulary and speaking clearly rather than worrying about your accent. Stay away from slang. But most importantly, think of your accent as cool. As an asset that gives you street credibility or access to a secret world where those who merely talk like the TV are forbidden entry. In the end, it's all about the attitude. Use your accent with clarity and confidence.

BIAS

This is a great time to play on the interviewer's cognitive biases, which are working overtime during this first meeting. Beyond your own presentation, there are common beliefs you can exploit to encourage people to think well of you far outside anything you've asserted directly or through your unconscious presentation. By offering something positive in these cases and leaving the rest open to interpretation, the interviewer is apt to make a better assumption of you than you could ever argue for yourself. So avoid the temptation to brag. Let them decide they are giving you their seal of approval instead of you trying to wrest it from them. They will trust their own assumption more and think better of you.

Exploit THE HALO EFFECT. Showcase your best attributes upon walking in the door. Because you have one positive attribute, people you meet will assume you have other positive attributes until proven otherwise.[20] (Fathers vetting daughters' dates might see the opposite, "the cloven-hoof effect" or something, where one flicked cigarette can spawn a vision of disaster and bedlam.) A useful effect of this halo is that it enables you access to things you might need, as described by Douglas Adams in *The Hitchhiker's Guide to the Galaxy*:

> A towel . . . is about the most massively useful thing an interstellar hitchhiker can have. Partly it has great practical value . . . More importantly, a towel has immense psychological value. For some reason, if a

strag [strag: non-hitchhiker] discovers that a hitchhiker has his towel with him, he will automatically assume that he is also in possession of a toothbrush, washcloth, soap, tin of biscuits, flask, compass, map, ball of string, gnat spray, wet-weather gear, space suit etc., etc. Furthermore, the strag will then happily lend the hitchhiker any of these or a dozen other items that the hitchhiker might have accidentally "lost."

Enhance your stereotypical self. The interview is a great time to exploit Confirmation Bias. Before the interview, ask yourself whether you look like you're right out of central casting for the job. "When people look at you, they see what they expect to see.... The more typical of a particular group you seem to be—the more you match others' ideas of what a member of a group should look, sound, and act like—the more strongly the stereotype will be applied to you."[21] What does this mean for you? First, learn which useful stereotypes fit both you and the situation, then milk them.

> People generally see what they look for, and hear what they listen for.
> —Harper Lee, *To Kill a Mockingbird*

For example, imagine an Ivy League legacy named Chase is cruising up to Sausalito to visit a firm he's been trying to get to invest in his tech company just prior to the IPO. He knows successful techbros are stereotyped as having Asperger syndrome so he works his hoodie and clipped diction and lets slip at the meeting—in a slightly squirrelly way—that in the early days, his programmer handle was "Zero." It works. A few weeks later, looking to buoy the new stock price, he pops across the country to a white-shoe firm on Wall Street. Wearing a proper suit, broad smile, and firm handshake he says, "call me Chase" and offers a nuanced opinion of who really ought to win the America's Cup this year. This also works. If you already seem like you fit in, they are likely to assume you fit in. On the other hand, if you are a brilliant ethnic-looking dude, don't tell the white-shoe boys your nickname is Sandy. If you embrace these easy-fit stereotypes when presenting yourself, you will seem more similar and familiar, two things which put people at ease. The important thing is to make sure no one who knows you as "Zero" runs into you acting like "Chase."

THE SCHIZOPHRENIC RESUME

You do not want to present a recruiter with a resume that's all over the place. Often seen as the result of too many interests, lack of focus, or a trust fund, a schizophrenic resume represents a person who might be bright but is also probably uncommitted, disloyal, crazy, and a pain in the ass. Regardless of other qualifications, the recruiter is likely to get a headache trying to make sense of the resume writer and simply toss the dissonant document. Of course, there are plenty of superstars with schizophrenic resumes out there, but try to remember, you are looking for a job, not flaunting your awesomeness. The recruiter's pathetic lack of imagination is not your concern. Chances are you've drifted from job to job more than most and your trajectory doesn't make easy sense in terms of goals and direction . . . so change it. Conform your old job descriptions to match the job you're looking to get. Instead of "convenience store stock boy," try "corporate cashier" when trying to land a job at a bank. At some point, HR will call to check on you, so avoid obvious lies like saying you were a manager at some place you've never even been to. Work on smaller "fixes." No one at 7-Eleven is going to remember exactly what your job description was last summer. Feather out your employment dates to cover idle time. Omit shady or drifty stuff, even if it was fun and cool at the time. Claim you graduated no matter what, and arrange for someone who doesn't sound like your best friend to give you a recommendation if called. If you get caught, and the chances are decent you will, tell the recruiter to chill the fuck out because you have evidence that 40 percent of all resumes are partially fabricated anyway.[22] You are just trying to get a fair shake in a cesspool full of liars.

PRACTICAL MATTERS

While you will be expending a good deal of energy on expressing yourself with cognitive coherence and basking in the glow of other people's assumptions, there is still some job-specific practical shit you must address during the interview. You'll need to show practical fitness, but don't worry, it matters less than you think.

THE SET UP. An important aspect of the interview is establishing your position, worth, and what you deserve. Some people say "take any job" just to get in the door, with the idea that you can wow your superiors later. But this is desperate advice. Your interviewer is paying more attention to you in the interview than he ever may again. He's trying to decide where you might fit into the organization. Stick to your guns and have a little self-respect. Demand the treatment you want up front. Remember, "an individual can more easily make a choice as to what line of treatment to demand . . . at the beginning of an encounter than he can alter the line of treatment . . . once the interaction is underway."[23] In many cases, you won't be hammering out the financial details with your new boss but at least make sure you're both clear and agreed on your position. Afterward, there will likely be some good cop/bad cop nonsense with HR or a manager trying to chisel you. Don't fall for it. Use your sociopathic gifts to hold your ground.

SHOPTALK. The specific terms, slang, and sometimes odd or esoteric language patterns employed by experts in any given field is shoptalk. Used correctly, shoptalk can give you instant authority with access, acceptance, and respect, because it shows you're down with the homies. But it's tricky. Even the slightest mistake can give you away. For example, in *Inglourious Basterds*, a British spy pretending to be German gives himself away by indicating "three" with three fingers—the British way—rather than the German way, with two fingers and the thumb. A tiny, deadly mistake. And it happens fast. People will give you street cred if you use shoptalk impeccably, but use it wrong, and you instantly look like a fraud and a dick. So err on the side of caution before throwing around specialty words you aren't fully confident of. Make an effort to learn them, they can help you. But also remember, shoptalk is a double-edged sword.

INVOKE THE BIG-PICTURE CLAUSE. When you don't know something specific or detailed, take evasive action. Say you're an idea man looking at the big picture. You leave it to the technicians to sweat the details. After all, you're a visionary, not just a wrist. Bold ideas are your forte. Try describing yourself as a comprehensive visionary type versus someone with a limited perspective. It's fun and effective.

Tip: That old antiperspirant ad was right. "Never let them see you sweat."

CHAPTER 5

PERSONALITIES

Is that crazy enough for ya? Want me to take a shit on the floor?
          —R. P. McMurphy, *One Flew Over the Cuckoo's Nest*

When you walk into the new job, your first order of business should be to identify the dominant psychological makeup of your coworkers and bosses. You need to understand what kind of sick mental stew you've stumbled into in order to operate effectively. The important thing is not to get bogged down by details. Don't get tripped up by the complexities of people. Stay above it and keep it simple. This chapter will show you how to break people down into clearly recognizable types and how to deal with them.

Because constant personality assessment can be exhausting, it's important to preserve your mental energy by quickly discerning who you need to pay attention to and who you can safely ignore. First, consider proximity. People you interact with often are going to form an opinion about you, which they will share freely, so those in close proximity should be studied carefully. Do your best to minimize being a cause for gossip. Second, identify the person as a TARGET, OBSTACLE, or FURNITURE. Everyone in the office is one of these. Targets are those you want to impress: pay attention. Obstacles are those who are actively in your way: pay attention. Furniture is everyone else: pay less attention.

Every person has a core operational style, which dictates how a person acts and reacts based on their deep-seated and often unconscious idea of themselves, or their psychological type. Supporting other peoples' ideas about themselves will ease tension. (The opposite is also true and can be quite an effective weapon.) This will help you navigate toward success with your true nature undetected. There is much truth to the statement—considered an indicator of High Machiavellianism—"the best way to handle people is to tell them what they want to hear."[1]

There are countless ways to define psychological types, usually highlighting the CENTRAL PREOCCUPATION at the core of the person you are trying to understand. This is the nugget, the subconscious focus of everything they do, the one thing most important to their identity. Often it will be something they're trying to hide, so look closely. Everyone will present a mixture of the following traits (for example, someone can be anxious *and* a slob) but try to pinpoint the weakness that worries them most and concentrate on that. Because there are so many types, I've listed the technical term in **CAPITALS** and hopefully a more evocative nickname in (parentheses) below.

ATTACHMENT STYLES

John Bowlby's pioneering research into early social development led to what's now known as "Attachment Theory" or, how your parents interacted with you as a child determines the way you will interact with others as adults. Attachment theory categorizes people based on the social distance or closeness they seek, the level of validation they need, and their general comfort level with other people. It's a convenient and powerful way to break down your peers and understand the best way to approach them regardless of subject, even bad news.

ANXIOUS ATTACHMENT (Validatees). This is the guy who always wears quirky shirts, hoping to elicit a cooing approval from the receptionist. He's the guy who races up to your desk, twitching and sweaty, if you don't respond to his "urgent" email within ten minutes. (They are *always* urgent emails). A personality nightmare, these people are best avoided. But since they represent about twenty percent of the population, you'll get stuck working with them. It's best to make them happy with tasks that are clearly defined, and have minimal "frightening gray areas" where abstract decisions need to be made (you will hear about each one in excruciating detail). Give them tasks that are likely to have frequent, concrete, and positive outcomes. For example, hand them a messy stack of folders. Tell them to neaten the papers up and arrange the folders in alphabetical order, not a lot of questions there. This activity will keep the validatee busy for a long time, the result will be easy to observe quickly, and the resulting neatness will make them feel satisfaction and positive reinforcement. If you get desperate, tell them to go pick up all the cigarette butts in the smoking yard, and make it seem important.

NORMAL ATTACHMENT (Even Steven). This is the coworker who gives you room when you're busy and nailing it, but speaks his mind and is open to different ideas. He's easy to work with, but difficult to control.

AVOIDANT (Hiders). They don't want your help and don't want you to ask for their help, either. Self-sufficient at best, or repressed and distant, you can't rely on them, but neither will they drag you down. It's best to leave them be, with a juicy, complex task. Just know that whatever it is you think they're thinking, that's not what they're thinking. But you won't know that until it's too late.

MOTIVATIONAL STYLES

E. Tory Higgins's *Theory of Regulatory Focus* divides people's motivations into two basic camps[2] based on what feels right or fits their natural sense of self.

PROMOTION FOCUS (Climbers). These people tend to be young, optimistic, and motivated by the potential for gain. This is the gal who says "we got this" and means it. Let her run as long as her path to success doesn't involve stepping on your neck.

PREVENTION FOCUS (Seat Belts). Generally older, these types may seem either boring or scared, but don't be quick to judge or discount them. Motivated to avoid risk, they hate to lose. Warren Buffet, investment Yoda, says "Rule number one: Never Lose Money."[3] Many successful entrepreneurs are highly risk averse.[4] Prevention-focused people are terrified of loss and relentlessly defend against it, always clipping coupons and hoarding pennies. This may seem to be cheap and pointless, but when you take into account they apply this tightfistedness to *every single thing* they do, it adds up over time. These are good people to use as fact checkers and accountants. They make fewer mistakes than most people and can be useful in monitoring your more elaborate ventures. Just be sure not to make them feel they're going out on a limb for any reason.

Please note that motivational style should not be confused with "the carrot versus the stick," which refers to methods used to try to get a jackass to shoulder the plow. Beating a jackass with the stick works OK, but makes him slow and hateful. If the carrot works as a reward, you will have a more motivated beast of burden. If you are working with non–literal jackasses, discovering the appropriate carrot which constitutes a meaningful and motivating reward can be time consuming and difficult. For this reason, it's useful to know research shows that if you demean people most of the time, but throw in some hard-won praise once in a while, perversely, people will respect you for it, and work as hard as they would for a fully positive reward.[5] Some call this judicious praise. It is devastatingly effective. If you have children and want to cripple them with anxiety, practice this method on them.

THE POWER OF SUBVERSION

One effective way to thwart those around you is to push them to do the opposite of what is comfortable and preferable to them.

KUZUSHI means "unbalancing" in martial arts and is considered the first step in taking down an opponent. Keep them off-balance as often as you can manage without implicating yourself as the aggressor. Someone off-balance is going to be bewildered, flustered, and defensive. Therefore not likely to attack. An effective way to undermine someone is to use the opposite of their understanding of a goal. To a climber suggesting a smart but risky trade, you could counter, "well, investing a quarter of that amount could be a positive way to minimize our exposure to risk across the board." In this way, you are quickly reclassifying his proposal for an inspired but speculative growth-potential idea into a defensive bid designed to round out your basket of funds. This will take the wind out of his sails. Going against a person's motivational style is a great way to shoot them down while appearing helpful. Remember, the easiest, smoothest way to advance is to figure out how to keep everyone else on their heels. Then, gently, soulfully remind them the worst is yet to come. Because it is.

REVERSE PSYCHOLOGY. If given the choice between two matched items "X" and "Y" and told, "don't pick X," studies show 76.5 percent of people will willfully choose "X," just because they were told *not* to. One postulated reason is that "to avoid greater future regret, individuals exhibit reactive behavior rather than compliance."[6] Meaning people feel shittier if they're wrong after doing what they were told to than they feel if they are wrong after they resisted. Weird but true. Remember this when you're trying to get a stubborn coworker to do what you want. "Whatever you do, Jimmy do *not* try to get that loan from Mr. Bean at Counter-Offer Bank. He's a mean bastard and will never give it to you." All the while, of course, Mr. Bean is giving you a cut of his commission.

WORLDVIEW

For those focused primarily on the universal "purpose of life," Plato's break-down of types can be quite useful.

PHILOSOPHERS (Wise Guys). Most interested in the meaning of things, they worry about "truth" and the purpose of our so-called reality. They are generally difficult to find in an office, as they would rather be walking naked up a mountain, chewing leaves. This is the dude with the ponytail who reads during lunch and will never give you a straight answer about anything. Wise guys are pretentious, difficult to fool, and motivated by neither the carrot nor the stick. Luckily, they are also relatively uninterested in the social world, have a terrible sense of fashion, and are generally underpaid and considered unfit for promotion. They are good at solving large, knotty problems, and can be used effectively to deal with intractable complications most people avoid. So if you can find one, throw them your most confusing shit and give them room to roam. They will neither disappoint nor upstage you.

SOLDIERS (Gunners). Motivated by honor and duty, these rare people are difficult to coerce or bribe, but are incredibly valuable in rallying the troops, creating social solidarity and defending the citadel. If you can win one over, they will stand by you when others doubt and abandon you. They're worthy allies and fight for morally upright ideals, but they can often get prickly and upset when you don't live up to your obligations. Do not lie to a gunner, and do not engage one, unless you are planning to execute what you represent as your intention. An angry gunner who doubts your intentions is a nightmare. On the other hand, one who buys into your shit is a better ally than you deserve.

LOVERS OF GRAIN (Slobs). Everyone else. These people are your bread and butter. They want shit. Stupid shit like a 2 percent raise or a donut. Some part of them believes that if they can someday drive a Beemer, they'll be able to cheat death. They actually care about what the Joneses are doing. Unfortunately, they are most people. But their hunger is the kind most easily fed, and feeding them puts them in your hands.

HELPING TYPES

If you see a man approach you with the obvious intent of doing you good, you should run for your life.

—Henry David Thoreau

Laid out by Adam Grant, PhD, these types are primarily concerned with the balance of effort put into a given project compared to the benefits received. Grant feels the most effective people over the long run are "disagreeable givers" but also wants to make sure you understand "that being a giver is not the same thing as being nice . . . nice guys and gals really do finish last."[7] Categorizing people in this way is most helpful when assessing underlings and potential hires.

GIVERS (Bounteous). People who are willing to give without expecting an equivalent return. Currently only 8 percent of people rate themselves as "givers" in the workplace. They "earn 14 percent less money, have twice the risk of becoming victims of crimes, and are judged as 22 percent less powerful and dominant."[8] No surprise there, but before you discount them as anything but a doormat, Adam also found top salesmen who were givers averaged "50 percent more annual revenue than the *takers* and *matchers*."[9] He claims that relentless givers and helpers "dominate both the bottom and the *top* of the success ladder." Done properly, giving can create reciprocity, the desire to return the favor. But you won't fall for that. For you, the interesting thing about the bounteous is that once they've done something to help you, the more likely they are to do it again.[10] They have already made a judgment about you as someone worthy to help, so they'll bend over backward to prove that their initial judgement was right. While the bottom group of givers are useless but easily worked, the top group is quite formidable. People are loyal to them. The best way to win a powerful giver over is to ask for help. Don't be squeamish. Successful people ask for help all the time.[11] Asking for help from a giver is the simplest way to get them to do what you want.

Tip: If you're ever in a position where giving a literal "gift" seems to be the best option, don't stress. You don't have to give something expensive. Studies show that giving extravagant gifts can quickly represent "conflict of interest" in the minds of the recipient (and the law) but, "gifts of negligible value can influence the behavior of the recipient in ways the recipient does not always realize."[12] Remember trading stickers in elementary school? Same idea, except the stickers were probably more valuable. The point is, you can influence a *surgeon* with a ballpoint pen or a coffee mug.

TAKERS (Gimme). These are the people angling for your office, the ones always looking out for themselves. They can be quite obvious about it to those below them, but are good at hiding it from their bosses or those in a position to help them. The phrase "kiss up, kick down" is what they chant in the mirror every morning while plucking their nose hairs. When not kissing ass, they're usually obnoxious, have expensive haircuts, and need to get in the last word about even the most stupid things like which freeze-dried instant coffee brand is the least disgusting. Life is easier when you can avoid takers, but they're quite common. A taker "kicking" you is irritating, but easy to read. A taker "kissing" you, however, is trickier to recognize, because they can be quite clever and deceitful. It's important to get a fix on them early, because once a gimme gets a taste, that sweet kiss will quickly knock you out.

MATCHERS (Time-Is-Money). These people are always keeping score. They remember when you took the last banana. They think of themselves as fair but are also kind of petty. On the upside, they are predictable.

WHAT TO DO WHEN YOU MEET ANOTHER YOU

Eventually, you will run into another sociopath (**Snake in the Grass**). This is a grave problem, and if you do need to take one head on, refer to chapter 13. Otherwise, do your best to not let him see you. Keep your interactions short and *don't* show any signs of weakness. If possible, have nothing to do with him. You want to stay the fuck away from people like you. Do not engage, just smile and walk away. If you're going to ignore this good advice, one fun thing to do with another sociopath is to get other people to recognize him for what he is. This will minimize his power. But *do not* make him your enemy. Be sly. You do not want him looking at you.

BRIBE TAKERS

These people are usually slobs who lurk around the break room hoping for treats. Most are useless and you shouldn't spend much mental energy on them. On the other hand, the bribes they require are cheap. Their loyalty is no match for a gunner's which makes them more like the "one night stand" variety of office allies. Somewhat useful to have in your back pocket, they can always buy you some time, but do not depend on them.

HUGS. A giver with low self-esteem. The fat girl. Don't lie and don't pretend to be shocked because I just said that. We all know her and have used her generosity more than once. At first glance, this person is a gift. They want to do things for you. They derive satisfaction from taking care of you because their personal life is a gaping void. This is all well and good when things are well and good. These people will make your life easier. But they also hate to deliver bad news and have a difficult time with failure, so when the road gets rough, they bullshit you and should not be trusted. They are often ingratiating and hold secret grudges. Do not give in to the temptation to surround yourself with them. The momentary ease and satisfaction they provide can later doom you with inept niceties.

DOUGHNUTS. Chocolates, cookies, flowers, these people are really into meaningless corporate holidays like Valentine's Day and can be bought off with a free lunch.

BENJI BOYS. Give 'em a raise. Or a sick day. Or a gift card to Applebee's. Always looking for money, they are smarter than the doughnuts, but not by much.

ALCOHOLICS. These sad sacks are a little more expensive to co-opt, as liquor is more expensive than a donut. But they are also usually open to your more shady or R-rated pursuits, especially after a few pickle-backs at happy hour. A functional alcoholic is not useless and can be kind of fun. Just don't tell him any secrets.

BACK CHANNELERS. A subpar version of the Validatee, this person will take your bribe but then talk viciously behind your back in order to make herself feel less like the piece of shit she is. She's the woman who undermines you in a meeting after agreeing with you all week. She cannot be trusted. Unfortunately, back channeling is a trait more commonly associated with females and brings to mind weakness, poison rings, and spells. She will cause you nothing but trouble. If the first person you want to avoid in the office is the snake in the grass, the back channeler is the second, and she is far more common.

Of course, a person is more complicated than any one of these reductive analyses, and can often reflect a kaleidoscope of different traits at the same time. But don't be dazzled. Look closer. You're not just pinning names on their behavioral flourishes, like some drunk psychic, you are looking for an *injury*. Through all the distracting light and noise, a person always hovers most closely to their deepest pet psychic wound, shielding it. This is the weakness in their story they tell to themselves. This is their central preoccupation, where they really feel fucked up. Find this place. Then, use your preternatural sociopathic coolness to pinpoint the character style the person employs to protect this wound. This is the personality style that matters; the one that protects the wounded self. If you can cater to this character style, the person will be putty in your hands.

An apparent matcher who holds dear the anger that his father drank away any inheritance he might have received should be treated as a true matcher. An apparent matcher who plays tough at the office as a means to keep everyone at arm's length because he doesn't trust anyone, should be treated as avoidant. Etcetera. You're clever, you'll get the hang of it. When in doubt, seek scars, wounds, and injuries.

CHAPTER 6
POWER

Paulo: Put your hands up!
Hans: No.
Paulo: What?
Hans: I said no.
Paulo: Why not?
Hans: Because I don't want to.
Paulo: But I've got a gun.
Hans: I don't care.
Paulo: That doesn't make any sense!
Hans: Too bad!

—Martin McDonagh, *Seven Psychopaths*

Power itself is a huge topic, but for the purposes of this book, we will look at two areas you will need to know in order to manipulate effectively. First is how to recognize who *really* has power and how to deal with them. Second is how people with power generally behave and why you should copy them.

POWER AROUND YOU

INFORMAL POWER. Formal power is the official hierarchy of any organization. There's probably a greasy laminated flow chart of it somewhere in an office drawer indicating who gets to step on the neck of whom. You should note your position to give yourself a sense of who is technically above and below you, as the most effective ways to treat the two groups differ markedly. But don't stop there. Of more importance is informal power. Who gets the best assignments? Who are their confidantes? Allies? Who sits in closed-door meetings? Who goes out for lunch or drinks together? Their formal position makes no difference. Those who are "in the meeting" have power. For example, a Harvard MBA may be on board to satisfy the clients' sense of propriety, but the favorite secretary actually understands what these clients need and is more valued by the CEO. You should treat all these people as if they have the same power level as the person who relies on them. If you disrespect them, you will quickly find yourself in trouble.

An early warning sign: if everyone around you seems to be doing things together which you're not invited to, you have offended someone, and unless you're in the self-sabotaging habit of messing with your boss, it's probably someone with informal power. Wolves isolate a deer before killing it. Your coworkers are doing this to you. You are in trouble and your only courses of action are to transfer immediately or make things right with the informal power player. Other forms of indirect power to keep an eye out for are legacy, kinship, "brotherhoods," and club affiliations.

It's worth your time to pinpoint the power positions of your coworkers regardless of title and be honest with yourself about your position relative to them. And remember, they're not necessarily going to be advertising their position. As Margaret Thatcher said, "Power is like being a lady . . . if you have to tell people you are, you aren't." You need to look for it. From there, you should modify your general tone depending on their position.

More Powerful, and You Need Them. These people are important. Get their attention and create an alliance. You'll want to make yourself useful and make them look good.

More Powerful, and You Don't Need Them. Avoid them as much as possible and work hard to undermine them. Help as necessary but also openly acknowledge their flaws and weaknesses to others.

Less Powerful, but You Need Them. Let them in on little secrets and make them feel important. It's good to build an alliance whenever possible—you never know who's going to get promoted.

Less Powerful, and You Don't Need Them. You can ignore them, but be careful when dismissing people you assume have no power. Remember the proverb: little pitchers have big ears. You always need more people than you think, and you can never be sure where a person is going or who they are talking to.

Use this information to remind yourself how to behave with each person as the need arises. The basic strategy is to pay as little attention to those you don't need while working for those you do. But at the same time, keep as many people on your side as possible.

THE GEOGRAPHY OF POWER

The corner office may sound like an eighties cliché but geographic power designations are very real and age-old phenomena. Where you sit in the company plan, at a restaurant, inside your office, or around the conference table really does have a tangible effect on your perceived power or how a proposal will be received.[1] Mafia dons are not the only ones to worry about getting shot from behind; almost everyone feels vulnerable when their back is to the door. Spatial intimidation has psychological effects on your opponent. Keep this in mind as you position yourself to exude maximum power. Sit in the higher chair, closer to the boss, and literally look down on everyone else.

GET ATTENTION

To secure a promotion, you need to attract positive notice from your bosses. But a classic problem with powerful people is getting them to pay attention to you. To do that effectively is not to tell them how great they are (they already know that) but how you can help them become even more great. According to psychologist Heidi Grant Halvorson, "It's not so much that they think they are better than you as it is they simply do not think about you at all. . . . To really get their attention, you'll need to let them know how *you* can help facilitate their continuing, increasing awesomeness."[2] If you can make them feel their power is totally justified and essential, and you are helping them wield it, they will pay attention. An opportune time for attracting attention is during activities where the power player is focused on an interpersonal task like brainstorming or team building. The powerful are more likely to pay attention to you at this time.[3] So suck it up and volunteer for those awful focus groups and do your best to cast yourself as instrumental in achieving positive results.

Because it is so difficult to get those in power to pay attention to you, make sure to avoid becoming the center of negative attention at all costs. Never deliver bad news. Get someone else to do it. Never volunteer to accept blame. Nothing is ever your fault. The problem is never you. Always someone else. Stick to this, always. And finally, before sticking your neck out to do something unusual, think twice. The adage "no good deed goes unpunished" has taken root for a reason.

GET CREDIT

Don't assume that just because you are doing a good job your superiors are aware of it. Remember, they aren't paying attention to you unless they have to. Highlight the complicated details involved in your work to make sure people understand you are busy. Learn to call attention to a result skillfully achieved and take as much credit as possible regardless of whether it's your work or not. Otherwise, no one will be impressed. Don't just think because a job is well done you will be recognized for it. People (especially those more powerful than you) don't think like this, and they are prone to absorb unclaimed praise into themselves, thinking "of course it's well done, *my* 'task force' (i.e., you) always does a good job because they work for me and I am seriously stupendous." Learn to dramatize your work so observers can see the results in real time. Even if you have to devise some busy-looking yet utterly irrelevant MAKE-WORK if you have to.

What is make-work? Have you ever seen that group of like nine construction workers standing around in an intersection on a double-time Sunday? Well if you stare at them long enough with a hateful "those are my tax dollars" look, the most sheepish one may well display a piece of make-work by say, measuring the width of a standard-issue K-rail that happens to be sitting there, or haphazardly marking an "X" on the ground with fluorescent spray paint. While you can surely do better than this, the point is that any display of effort will make people more appreciative of the work you are doing. President

Trump is a master of transforming any activity into a show. He could probably turn *America's Top Data Entry Clerk* into a reality hit. Social psychologist Erving Goffman says, "Those who have the time and talent to perform a task well may not . . . have the time or talent to make it apparent that they are performing well."[4] Don't let that be you.

Look at Edison versus Tesla. Who invented the alternating current we use today? Tesla. Whose failed direct current led to the first—and gruesomely botched—electric chair execution? Edison. Even so, Edison gained control of the AC patent and plastered his name on every power station, lightbulb, and invention he pried away from other people. Who died a forgotten, crazy, and penniless dude in a bum hotel who liked to feed pigeons? Tesla. (Well, some claim he flew to Mars instead.) And this happened even though he was a futurist idealistic genius and the first to envision our current wireless society. If you're lucky enough to have brilliance like Tesla carve out some time to advertise and brag about yourself. Don't be a Tesla.

Tip: The easiest way to move up the power structure is to find someone high up and get them to like you. Make them depend on you. Many people make the mistake of being jealous of a person moving quickly up through the ranks, but if you can get close instead, you can draft[5] in his wake with less friction, like sticking close to a semi on the freeway.

POWER BEHAVIOR

The old saw says that power corrupts, and while you may well object to attaching the negative connotations of "corrupts" to "power," the point is that the psychological and behavioral effects of power are immediate, intense, and self-perpetuating. Power is important. You should know how it is routinely expressed so you can react properly and present yourself as powerfully as possible. As with confidence, acting powerful cannot be overrated. Act powerful and people will believe you.

BEING A DICK

Countless studies have found that people given even a tiny increase in power immediately become more of a dick. They "start talking more, taking what they want for themselves, ignoring what other people say or want, ignoring how less powerful people react to their behavior, acting more rudely, and generally treating any situation or person as a means for satisfying their own needs."[6] The research shows that acting like this also makes people believe you actually are more powerful. Furthermore, the more powerful you get, the more powerful you act. It's a self-perpetuating, self-fulfilling dick wag. What these studies tell us is that being a dick can be very effective.[7]

These studies also show that "being put in positions of power blinds them to the fact that they are acting like [a dick]."[8] But this alleged obliviousness is just part of the story. The dicks may say they don't notice their own uptick in dickish behavior, but outside the lab, workplace field tests show dicks are *highly* aware upon whom they unleash their dickishness. Fifty to 80 percent of "nastiness is directed by superiors to their subordinates . . . with somewhat less between coworkers of roughly the same rank (20 percent to 50 percent) and "upward" nastiness—where underlings take on their superiors—occurs in less than 1 percent of cases."[9] So dicks are clearly aware of what they're doing. To most effectively harness the power of being a dick, these numbers are a good rule of thumb to keep in mind. If you're being a dick to a subordinate no one will think it's

particularly notable—just typical kiss-up, kick-down behavior—but if you are looking at a 1 percent situation, beware. You might be making a big mistake.

The Difference Between Dicks, Assholes, Jerks, and You. These aggressive types still suffer from moral reasoning and empathy. Do not confuse someone asserting their dominance or aggression with them being a sociopath. This is a common mistake, and one that is potentially energy draining for you. You're going to have to deal with enough bona fide sociopathic competitors along the way, so don't gum up your defensive apparatus with a bunch of mere dicks. Don't give them that much credit. They're still going to go back to their car and cry when no one's looking. Adam Grant found that many people rate themselves as givers in relationships while unlikely to call themselves the same at work.[10] These hard-nosed executives can afford to turn into pussycats once they hit their front gate. You don't have that luxury.

BEING SENSITIVE

That said, it is also wise to think twice about when to be a dick. Astute superiors may well keep an eye on how you treat people with no power, seen by many as a strong indication of character. (For example, Goethe wrote: "You can easily judge the character of a man by how he treats those who can do nothing for him.") Try to resist the urge to kick down unless you need to target a specific threat, in which case it is best to isolate the person first and make sure no superiors can see you. At that point, have fun. Isolating is an incredibly useful tool when cutting to pieces someone who is climbing to power. When in doubt, isolate. Once you have some power it can sometimes be effective (and fun) to stage a well-timed temper tantrum in full view to motivate your lazy lackeys, but never abandon your old, effective friends: deprivation and isolation.

TRUE CONFESSIONS

"Power is all I have ever really cared about in my life: physical power, the power of being desired or admired, destructive power, knowledge, invisible influence. I like people. I like people so much that I want to touch them, mold them, or ruin them however I'd like. Not because I want to witness the results, necessarily, but simply because I want to exercise my power."

—M. E. Thomas, *Confessions of a Sociopath*

TERRITORIAL PISSING

This won't surprise you. A study adeptly titled "Territorial Defense in Parking Lots: Retaliation Against Waiting Drivers" shows people will take longer to leave a parking spot when someone is waiting for the spot than when no one is waiting.[11] Some argue that a distraction factor needs to be taken into account in this case, but there is also evidence that men will still move more slowly—but to a lesser degree—if the waiting car is a high-status vehicle. This means they're being more deferential to the higher-status person while still also being a dick. This is insanely petty but it shows you the baseline of where people are at when they have no need to be bonded to the other person in any meaningful way. (Think about road rage.) People are perfectly willing to act out when there is no perceived consequence. Remember this if someone seems shocked by something you did. Shrug it off and say, "I didn't know anyone was looking" or "You would have done the same thing in my situation."

WATCH YOUR MOUTH

Your vocabulary is an indicator of status, but not in ways you might suspect. According to language expert James W. Pennebaker in *The Secret Life of Pronouns*, you convey power not necessarily through a big impressive vocabulary, but rather with how you use small connecting words (such as *we, you, to, for, but*, and *not*) which "account for less than one-tenth of 1 percent of your vocabulary but make up almost 60 percent of the words you use." Pronouns are perhaps the most revealing of this group. For example, "contrary to what most people think, high-status people tend to use *we* and *you* at high rates compared to lower-status individuals. . . . And low-status individuals overuse *I*.[12] The most common word in the English language is *I*, and overusing it can also signal that you are insecure, self-focused, and depressed. Conversely, the more powerful you are, the more likely you are to use articles and prepositions along with your big vocabulary. So, before you hit send, double-check your emails for excessive *I*s and pronouns. Never send an email reply like "I think I gave it to them."

Because is an extremely effective word you should employ often. People react strongly to the word regardless of whether or not the reason following it has any merit whatsoever. Just saying *because* enables you to cut in line at a 50 percent higher rate. Here is Ellen Langer's[13] experiment. There's a line at the copier. You say, "Excuse me, I have five pages. May I use the Xerox?" Sixty percent of people will let you cut in. If you say "Excuse me, I have five pages. May I use the Xerox *because* I'm in a rush?" Then, 94 percent of people let you cut in. You assume the uptick in civic generosity to be because you have a valid, pressing reason. But that's not the case. If you say, "Excuse me, I have five pages. May I use the Xerox *because I need to make copies*," 93 percent of people will *still* let you cut in even though your reason is totally vacuous. This is how Donald Trump replied when asked about who he's consulting with on serious foreign policy concerns: "I'm speaking with myself, number one, *because* I have a very good brain and I've said a lot of things." Critics might call this empty rhetoric but that's their problem. If it helps you, *because* it provides a positive outcome for you, it's not so empty, is it?

Tip: In certain situations, casual swearing totally works as a symbol of dominance.

Generalize. It helps diffuse the power of individual experience. *Never* and *always* are good words to strengthen just about any assertion. If you're going to say something totally false, state it confidently with these types of words, as in "I always wash my hands after going to the bathroom." Conversely, qualifying words like *probably* are weak and useless and you should strike them from your vocabulary immediately, and never, ever, qualify yourself.

Short, direct statements are more easily understood and remembered. If you want to make a point, say it succinctly and directly. If you want to obscure a fact, use big words. As George Orwell said, "The inflated style itself is a kind of euphemism. A mass of Latin words falls upon the facts like soft snow, blurring the outline and covering up all the details. The great enemy of clear language is insincerity. When there is a gap between one's real and one's declared aims, one turns as it were instinctively to long words and exhausted idioms, like a cuttle-fish spurting out ink."[14]

YOUR OWN POWER

Here are some fun final pieces of advice from the eighties book, *Power! How to Get It. How to Use It*:

"Don't ask for favors. Grant them willingly enough but make sure there's no way of returning them. Act with impassive, but instinctive generosity."

"The busier you can make yourself, the more you can impose your schedule on other people, the more power you have."

"The guy who has the power is the one who walks in empty-handed. The ones with the attaché cases are spear carriers ..."

The trappings of power may seem like silly, empty formalities, but do not disregard or shrug them off as stupid and pointless. They are extremely important; people don't want to waste their own time deciding who you are or whether they should risk their own reputation by vouching for you. Amassing power is difficult, but the first steps are simple and direct. Make it your business to recognize all kinds of power. Get yourself noticed in a positive light by those in power. Get credit, take the title. Act powerful. People will believe you.

PART TWO

GETTING UP

CHAPTER 7

CREATE AN EFFECTIVE CHARACTER

There will be time
To prepare a face to meet the faces that you meet:
There will be time to murder and create
                              —T. S. Eliot, "The Love Song of J. Alfred Prufrock"

You are reasonably well-hidden and functional in society, which means you have learned the logical meaning of the major emotions, what they look and sound like, and when and how they are appropriately expressed. You are generally understood to be able to pantomime emotions but not experience them directly.[1] You've practiced and effectively displayed expressive coherence at your interview. Now you need to extend this coherence over a longer period of time and it's the performance of your life. The good news is, you are better at pretending than the average person.[2]

TRUES CONFESSIONS

I'm a tenderhearted motherfucker. I'm 'raw' and 'wounded' and expend a decent amount of energy every day to make it seem that way. Expressing weakness is a great way to elicit empathy and get people to let down their guard.
                              —T. Johnson, pilot. Bridgeport CT

In the office, the depth of your inner feeling doesn't matter, as long as you seem okay and reasonably consistent and collected. Do you think people at work actually care who you are at heart? Do you think they care if you unleash your sociopathic side at home or at the bar none of them go to? No. Because they don't want to think about you at all. They want to feel secure enough in the fact that you won't fuck them over that they can stop worrying about you altogether. So they can forget about you and think about themselves. I'm not saying there aren't great-hearted men and women in business who form deep collaborations, connections, alliances, and loyalty to one another, striving forth with excellence and providing meaningful contributions to society. Blah, blah, blah. I'm just saying you're not one of them. And I'm trying to help you.

A SENSE OF SELF

While you've been described as wearing a "mask of sanity," it's essential to understand that everyone else is *not* walking around with some immutable and ironclad sense of "who they really are" and an assured sense of self and identity. Everyone around you is also wearing a mask, also playing a "character," if for different reasons. The very word *person* comes from the Latin word "persona" or "mask." There is no "self" that is flawlessly innate and natural and able to shift from private to public spheres without any acting. Everybody acts. And everybody acts differently all day long, depending on who they're with and what they're selling.

"All the world's a stage" just about says it all. Shakespeare may be so enduringly popular because he can express the hollowness most people feel, even if they spend their lives hiding it. "Life is but a walking shadow, a poor player that struts and frets his hour upon the stage and then is heard no more. It is a tale told by an idiot, full of sound and fury, signifying nothing."[3]

Here are some other interesting quotes about self, to give you a flavor of what other people feel like inside. You may be cooler, emptier, but you're not completely different.

> "We may practically say he has as many different social selves as there are distinct groups of persons about whose opinion he cares. . . . Many a youth who is demure enough before his parents and teachers, swears and swaggers like a pirate among his 'tough' young friends."
>
> —William James, *The Principles of Psychology*

"We are things that labor under the illusion of having a self; an accretion of sensory experience and feeling, programmed with total assurance that we are each somebody, when in fact everybody is nobody."

—Rust Cohle, *True Detective*

"Facts about ourselves are not particularly solid and resistant to skeptical dissolution. Our natures are, indeed, elusively insubstantial—notoriously less stable and less inherent than the natures of other things. And insofar as this is the case, sincerity itself is bullshit."

—Harry G. Frankfurt, *On Bullshit*

"A man's at odds to know his mind cause his mind is aught he has to know it with."

— Cormac McCarthy, *Blood Meridian*

"We are unknown, we knowers, to ourselves. . . . Of necessity we remain strangers to ourselves, we understand ourselves not, in ourselves we are bound to be mistaken, for each of us holds good to all eternity the motto, 'Each is the farthest away from himself'—as far as ourselves are concerned we are not knowers."

—Friedrich Nietzsche, *The Genealogy of Morals*

"Most people love you for who you pretend to be. To keep their love, you keep pretending-performing. You get to love your pretense. It's true, we're locked in an image, an act—and the sad thing is, people get so used to their image, they grow attached to their masks. They love their chains. They forget all about who they really are. And if you try to remind them, they hate you for it, they feel like you're trying to steal their most precious possession."

—Jim Morrison, *Creem* magazine

"I'm beginning to know myself. I don't exist. . . . I'm the gap between what I'd like to be and what others have made of me. Period."
—Fernando Pessoa, *The Book of Disquiet*

AT REST

Dexter, the serial killer star of the show *Dexter*, is able to evade detection for as long as he does because of his father's teachings on how best to hide his "dark passenger." He adopts a resting persona that's sort of an affable vanilla. This is a good strategy for your everyday behavior. You want to seem relaxed yet confident. You don't want to stand out as too peculiar, but also don't want to come across as a boring wallflower. Most importantly, you need a safe resting stance to hide your inappropriate sociopathic urges, a persona which doesn't exhaust you with excessive control requirements. You don't need to be the big-hearted office confidant, but you do need, at least, to make sure you don't kill animals at work.

Hide early and often. Divert suspicion. It's easier to keep suspicion from cropping up than it is to quell it once it has been aroused. Remember, "Good people are rarely suspicious: they cannot imagine others doing things they themselves are incapable of doing."[4] Most people lack imagination. It takes a lot to make them suspicious. They may be an exasperatingly easy target, but you need to learn to resist the urge to go out of your way to menace them. For God sakes, keep ahold of yourself.

When pursuing advancement and power, you will at times be required to assert your fitness for promotion, which may well require a more active persona. If your expressive coherence is in good working order, you can turn on a more proactive and aggressive character to solidify and improve your position. Then return to your affable vanilla to rest.

Sociopaths tend to overwhitewash their shortcomings. Resist the temptation to make yourself look too good. It will make people suspicious. By allowing yourself to exhibit a few weaknesses you'll come off as more personable. Create a weird hobby for yourself that no one else is interested in. For example, tell people you collect vintage 8 mm home movies from thrift shops. No one will ever want to watch them with you, nor will they doubt you do this at night, and will think watching must take a lot of time and patience. A perfect alibi.

Tip: Army training for British Special Forces includes how to act when captured. The tactic is to become the "gray man" and make yourself as bland and featureless as possible.[5] To seem unimportant and irrelevant works as psychological camouflage. While not exactly a getting-ahead strategy, it's something to keep in mind for when you are next feeling vulnerable.

OFFICE PARTIES

Sociopaths, alcohol, dates, and bosses present a potentially dangerous combination. But suck it up and be smart. Properly utilized, the holiday party offers a three-way goldmine: you can display and expand your agreeable persona, maneuver though power channels that aren't normally open to you, and pick up a double-edged secret or two once everybody's drunk.

Circulate with robust good cheer like an agreeable, promotable asset. A team player. If you can swing it, borrow, beg, or steal a hilarious and hot date to provide cover and make you look cool, even if you are never going to sleep together. Otherwise, come alone. Don't overdress and don't act excited about the free booze and food. This behavior is for plebes. The food will be awkward to eat, so skipping it altogether is safest, though clumsily trying to wrangle a Swedish meatball on a tiny plastic sword can provide some comic relief and make you seem endearing to your peers.

The office party offers a unique opportunity to strike up a conversation with those above you who you might not normally have access to. Everyone is slightly out of their element, so the game is looser than at the office. But you need to make sure you strike at the right time. In *Power! How to Get It, How to Use It*, author Michael Korda gets technical with office party power maneuvers. I'll roughly paraphrase. Those in power will come late and leave early. At 00:00 the first wave of sheep arrive, excited about the buffet, the booze, and having a jolly time. 00:30 the rest arrive, playing it a little more nonchalant. This is when you should come in. 00:40 the bosses start to show up, to talk to their workers. 00:55 the bosses will clump together and talk to each other. During which time everyone else is assessing who is talking to whom, and who's garnering a crowd. It's a big time for posturing beneath the good cheer. Bide your time. The sweet spot for interlevel hobnobbing is the second hour after the party starts.[6] The boss clump will dissolve, indicating a hierarchical free-for-all. Just make sure to wait until those above you are finished saying hello to those above them. Then you should drop in for a quick, breezy conversation with a superior you want to impress.

Don't get drunk and dance on desks. On the other hand, refraining from drinking at all will make people think you're an alcoholic, so drink some beer. The third hour is a great time to glean compromising information that can be useful later. Think of a party as a fact-finding mission. Be professional when no one else is. People will get drunk and let down their guard. Ask questions, listen. Keep your wits about you. This is especially effective when you are dealing with those who wield indirect power.

Because drunk people often act like idiots, people who see you with a drink are proven to think you are stupider than if you weren't holding a drink . . . even if you exhibit zero evidence of being impaired. Studies find that "in the absence of any evidence of reduced cognitive performance, people who hold an alcoholic beverage are perceived to be less intelligent than those who do not, a mistake we term the imbibing idiot bias."[7] This is good cover. Carrying a drink will make you seem like less of an inquisitive threat. Once people get uselessly sloppy, go home. Don't announce you're going. Just leave.

NATURALNESS

People fake a lot of human interactions, but I feel like I fake them all, and I fake them very well. That's my burden, I guess.

—Dexter, *Dexter*

Naturalness is an extension of expressive coherence, and people are very attentive to any breaks or hiccups in the routine. Being natural is unconscious and easy. Acting natural is quite difficult. In *The Presentation of Self in Everyday Life*, Erving Goffman suggests people are better equipped to sniff out a fraud than be a convincing actor, saying "the arts of piercing an individual's effort at calculated unintentionality seem better developed than our capacity to manipulate our own behavior." So this is a bind; you're a total fraud required to perform—for an extended period of time—a believable character for people who are great at one thing: recognizing a fraud. So what are you supposed to do?

Actors have all sorts of tricks to create a convincing natural character. Michael Caine says, "While rehearsing something with a fellow actor, if a crew member can come up and recognize you're rehearsing versus having a real conversation, then you aren't doing it right." Method actors tie themselves up in psychic knots following the Meisner technique to "live truthfully under given imaginary circumstances" or gain "complete emotional identification with a part." Michael Chekhov students work in earnest to improve their proprioception and focus on "mind, body and a conscious awareness of the senses." [8] But it doesn't have to be this hard.

You can affect the look of an emotional state without feeling it at all. For example, James Franco keeps it simple. To invoke his famous enigmatic grin, he doesn't think about a long-lost love or the meaning of the universe. He says, "Sometimes I'm imagining a fan blowing hot air on me. And sometimes I imagine it's a blast of bus exhaust."[9] Johnny Depp keeps it complicated. A quote attributed to him online: "I try to stay in a constant state of confusion just because of the expression it leaves on my face."[10] It's worth exploring what weird random thoughts can give you that "I'm a normal, nice-ish person" face, and use them. Because, as Marlon Brando well knew, "it is a simple fact that all of us use the techniques of acting to achieve whatever ends we seek. . . . Acting serves as the quintessential social lubricant and a device for protecting our interests and gaining advantage in every aspect of life."[11]

Perry, one of the killers in Truman Capote's *In Cold Blood,* used the mirror to help him create different expressions: "It was a changeling's face, and mirror-guided experiments had taught him how to ring the changes, how to look now ominous, now impish, now soulful; a tilt of the head, a twist of the lips, and the corrupt gypsy became the gentle romantic."[12] Many actors use mirror work to perfect their characters' expressions and gestures. Mirrors are everywhere. Practice and learn what your face looks like.

If your acting chops don't seem up to the conversation at hand, do your best to get off stage. Ask people about themselves, *Homo sapiens* love talking about themselves. Take an interest in the world around you or otherwise divert attention away from your performance.

CONFIDENCE IS NOT ARROGANCE

Matt Damon, playing up the appeal of his Jason Bourne character, has an uncommon view of the world's most famous spy: "They could never make a James Bond movie like any of the Bourne films . . . because Bond is an imperialist, misogynist sociopath who goes around bedding women and swilling martinis and killing people. He's repulsive." Whatever, Matt. He's also one of the most popular heroes of the last fifty years. And he has way more fun than Bourne, who, let's face it, is kind of a sucker.

General Patton used to practice his impressive scowl in front of the mirror for hours. For many, confidence is difficult to muster and project. Not for you, but this doesn't mean you won't have a confidence problem if you're not careful. Motivational speaker Walter Bond frames it in a way that's particularly useful for you: "Confidence is arrogance under control." Control is the operative word here. Take this Bond's advice and keep a muzzle on your arrogance. Confidence and arrogance invoke very different responses in others.

DON'T GET COCKY

Not everyone is burdened with disguising the fact that they're a sociopath, but they do perform normalized roles for one another all the time in order to make society function smoothly. Whether acting as doctor, waitress, teacher, friend, or husband, their elaborate psychosocial contract works only because they agree to believe each other. They offer what Goffman describes as PROTECTIVE PRACTICES: people are desperate not to make a scene, so they'll go to great lengths to support the validity of your asserted self in order to avoid public embarrassment. Even if they can see right through your act.

This is important for you to remember when you seem to really be pulling it off. It's not just because you are doing such a dazzling job. It's not just because you're smarter and better than everybody else. It's partly because the people around you are offering to believe you, in the name of keeping order. Goffman says, "Few impressions could survive if those who received the impression did not exert tact in their reception of it." This is a good thing to keep in mind, when your feelings of ruling, and winning, and killing it, are running hot. You're not fooling everyone as much as they're letting you believe.

Similarly, BLINDSPOT BIAS leads you to believe other people's judgement is clouded by their biases, while your own judgement is not. Not true. In general, we notice flaws in others more easily than we notice them in ourselves, which is a weakness. Narcissists take note: this is especially true for *you*. You are consistently the worst offenders, even though you're probably disagreeing vigorously right now. Trust me, your blind spot is *large*.[13]

It's worth repeating: don't get cocky. This is how mistakes are made. You're not *that* good. People are constantly giving you a break and will continue to do so until it becomes more uncomfortable for them to ignore your bullshit than to openly confront you.

Here are some amazing examples of Silicon Valley techbros who just can't help themselves. Usually, they get a pass for acting like an overt sociopath because investors want to believe their "unicorn company" will make everyone involved stinking rich. That is, until the moment one of these bros gets the genius idea to force into the open just how undeniably awful he is.

Self-described "entrepreneur" and San Francisco resident, Justin Keller took it upon himself to write an amazingly ill-conceived public letter to the San Francisco mayor and chief of police. Unprompted, he wrote, "I know people are frustrated about gentrification happening in the city, but the reality is, we live in a free market society. . . . The wealthy working people have earned their right to live in the city. . . . I shouldn't have to see the pain, struggle, and despair of homeless people to and from my way to work every day." What was the fucking point of writing that? Now, this previously undercover operator is world-famous for being a narcissistic clueless prick, hated by everybody. Stupid move.

Then of course, there's Martin Shkreli the (self-described, I believe) "pharmabro," who raised the price of the life-saving AIDS drug Daraprim from $13.50 a pill to $750 a pill. He could have tried to soothe the ensuing uproar with the dickish but somewhat legitimate arguments he used later; that pharma has a legal right to charge whatever it wants for a privately studied and licensed product, or that the drug prices of today pay to develop the drugs for tomorrow, etc. But he didn't even do that. Instead, he sat in front of Congress on national television, smirked, rolled his eyes, and pleaded the fifth with such bratty contempt that even people who hate Congress immediately shifted all that hate onto this dude. Since then convicted for securities fraud, this bro obviously doesn't know how to play his cards right and has no idea how to be cool. He is not your role model.

Don't say or do things like this. Keep your shit together. Pay attention to who you're talking to and don't put anything arrogant and stupid in writing, anywhere, ever.

Natural, affable, confident. If not exactly the building blocks of an exhilarating megastar, these are the traits you—as a sociopath—should keep in mind while creating your public face. Focus on maneuverability, creating space, and avoiding suspicion. Encourage people's instinct toward protective practices to work in your favor. Encourage them to protect you. Then strike when nobody's looking.

CHAPTER 8

DISGUISE AND RECHARGE

The mind is its own place, and in itself can make a heaven of hell, a hell of heaven.

—John Milton, *Paradise Lost*

Do you ever come home so tired from manipulating your coworkers that you can no longer do the same to your wife and children? Too tired to gaslight your wife into thinking she's crazy to think you're banging the totally hot and slutty nanny? It's because you're working too hard. No one can be "on" all the time and all this acting takes work. You need to preserve some energy.

One of the most difficult things for you is keeping up with appearances, day in, day out, over the long haul. It's understandable. Being charming to idiots gets soul-crushingly dull after a while and perseverance is something you find difficult. It's your weak flank. But, when you reach that point when you're sick to death of chatting with Old Mister Droog about his inane farting dog and can hardly restrain yourself from throwing a vase at his head, remember, perseverance is essential. Narcissists, you will be happy to know, you have an easier time of it than other sociopaths.

Being a talented sociopath is about being in control. At the end of the day, the difference for you between talented and fucked is self-control. As researcher Roy F. Baumeister has found, willpower is a limited resource.[1] So, you must pick your battles and preserve your energy. The more effort you expend running your resting character, the more likely you will leak your sociopathic tendencies at inopportune moments, because your self-control is exhausted. At this point, you feel like the fat man who's been snarfing carrot sticks all week and is now staring down a bacon double cheeseburger, and it sucks. Impatient, edgy, and ready to blow is no way to go through life.

TRUE CONFESSIONS

"I try to keep myself personally running smooth, you know, but some people can be irritating. The ones with all the questions about this little shit and that—you know they're not going to buy—but they keep asking about stupid seat heaters and shit. Well, anyways if I'm around one of them and I feel myself getting ready to freak the fuck out, I just excuse myself and go to the bathroom for a minute. A little self-love, you know, and you can cool out real quick. Then you can come back and you can deal."

—Mike Lee, car sales. Providence, Rhode Island

Mike is right. If you're about to yell at someone, you should just go masturbate instead.

PRESERVING ENERGY AND MINIMIZING EXPOSURE

Extending the shelf life of your self-control depends on knowing when to expend yourself and when you can relax.

LOVE THY NEIGHBOR. Proximity breeds exposure. The people you are around most often may not seem important to your getting ahead. But, they are most likely to witness a sociopathic slipup of yours, which could leak to just about anyone. Remember, you never know who's got a back channel to the boss. Be especially vigilant in controlling yourself around your cubicle-mates, neighbors, and daily contacts. Even if they have no power, they are worth your attention. It may seem like a waste of time, but trust me, it's worth currying their favor. If you can win them over, they will be more forgiving of the nasty outbreaks that do occur. It's easier than you think.

When there's nothing at stake, people tend to pick out things that are different about you, and react negatively (look at the amazing, pointless vitriol of Internet trolls) but, if you are *all in the same boat*, people will be motivated to find things to like about you, in the spirit of self-survival and cooperation. Studies show, "whether familiarity leads to liking or contempt crucially depends on our motivation."[2] So, the more you can project being part of the team, and the less you can expose your differentness, the more likely you'll be seen in a positive light by those crowding your space. Similar to the halo effect (assuming someone with one good quality will have other good qualities) it's a common belief that "people who are similar to me in one way are probably similar to me in other ways."[3] Exploit this. One simple way is to use cooperative and connecting phrases, like "I hear you," "me too," and "we *got* this."

LET GO. Learn how to relax and carve out time to turn off your self-control and learn to recognize when exercising your true nature is pointless. It will help you let it go more easily. You don't need to be Machiavellian in a restaurant. You're gonna get what you want anyway. You ordered a beer. You'll get a beer. You don't have to manipulate the waitress into bringing you one. Beyond requiring less energy, it's also smart. Not being over-the-top about exerting pressure lowers your exposure risk. For example, if you're out with a colleague you are intending to manipulate and inadvertently use one of your manipulation techniques on the waitress, your colleague could notice the similarity and get wise to you. Learn to relax in situations you don't need to control.

Also, learn to recognize things you cannot control. There's a reason the serenity prayer by Reinhold Nieburhr is beloved by Alcoholics Anonymous, another group who struggles with self-control:

God, grant me the serenity to accept the things I cannot change,
Courage to change the things I can,
And wisdom to know the difference.

Well, maybe skip the asking God for help part, but remember, if you can't control it, just relax. Let shit happen because it's going to anyway. Don't struggle uselessly against larger forces. It's a waste of time and energy.

> ## TRUE CONFESSIONS
> "You see, what you're calling coercion there, honey, I call taking charge. Domination? How about 'making decisions'? Manipulation? Nah, I'm just gifted at getting others to do what I want. That's why I got elected."
> —Beau Bunnyfriend, councilman, New Orleans.

MAKE A PRIVATE SPACE. If you've ever worked in a restaurant, you know well the difference in vibe between the kitchen and the dining room. This is the difference between a public space and a private space, and the fancier the place, the bigger the difference. Up front the public sees smiles, crisp linen, and polished knives. But in back it's hot and hurried, cussy, and no one thinks twice about grabbing a steak off the greasy floor. As George Orwell wrote after working as a dishwasher, "It is an instructive sight to see a waiter going into a hotel dining room. As he passes the door a sudden change comes over him. The set of his shoulders alters; all the dirt and hurry and irritation have dropped off in an instant. He glides over the carpet, with a solemn priest-like air."[4]

Everybody needs a kitchen, or a man cave. This is especially true for you. This is very important—you need a place where you can shore up your flagging sense of self-control. Find a place where you can retire to and relax, which is out of sight. Maybe it's your private office (though a closed office door is always noticed and causes speculation) but needn't be. A habitual post-lunch walk around the block can provide a great private space, so long as you make it a seemingly mundane routine, doing it even on days when you don't feel you need it, so as not to arouse curiosity on the days when you do. In Victorian times, a place to retreat to when in a nasty mood was known as a growlery. As Charles Dickens writes in *Bleak House*, "This, you must know, is the growlery. When I am out of humor, I come and growl here."

Hollywood is full of creative sociopaths who make unusual private space for themselves.[5] In fairy tales, heroes sometimes carry some kind of magic satchel, which can hold things much bigger than the satchel itself. Jack (of beanstalk fame) hid from the giant inside one of these. In *Harry Potter,* Hermione stashes a beaded handbag in her sock, which holds enough supplies for an entire camping expedition. The appeal of a tiny thing able to hold a big thing is great. To relieve his blood pressure, one Hollywood manager, sometimes known as the "Pink Yeller" bought himself a thick leather bag and called it his shouting bag. When he needed to spew hate, he would unburden himself by shouting into the bag, then close it up. The words were muffled by the bag, he felt a lot better, and no one could understand what was said.

In the 1970s, a character actor brought his own trailer to set. He called it the mayhem room. The trailer looked ordinary, but was both soundproof and armored inside. Between setups, the actor would "retire" to his trailer and smash shit to smithereens inside. He would shatter bottles and glasses, plates, and televisions with a baseball bat, then return to set rejuvenated, relaxed, and in control.

"To care only for well-being seems to me positively ill-bred. Whether it's good or bad, it is sometimes very pleasant, too, to smash things."
—Fyodor Dostoyevsky, *Notes from the Underground*

Make sure your private space has a warning system, so you have time to get your shit together, before someone sees you as you really are. This is what secretaries outside your door are for. If you don't have one of these, a security camera will work, but is generally seen as creepy and low-rent. In ancient Japan, samurais had the floors in their palaces engineered to squeak loudly any time someone walked across them. Known as nightingale floors, these floors would raise the alarm of even the stealthiest intruder in a pitch-black room. While you're not going to reengineer your floors, other noisemakers can come in handy, like bells on the door or blocking the route into your private space with a squeaky-wheeled mail cart. Get a cute dog who will bark when visitors arrive. He'll also make you seem like a kinder, gentler person. Use the tools available in your environment. It can be fun.

Here's a last word from Orwell on alarms. "All the discipline of the hotel depended on the manager. He was a conscientious man, and always on the lookout for slackness, but we were too clever for him. A system of service bells ran through the hotel, and the whole staff used these for signaling to one another. A long ring and a short ring, followed by two more long rings, meant the manager was coming, and when we heard it we took care to look busy."[6]

MISDIRECTION

> Attention is like water. It flows. It's liquid. You create channels to divert it, and you hope that it flows the right way. . . . Grift sense is the closest thing to a sixth sense we have. It's stepping outside yourself and seeing through the other person's eyes, thinking through the other person's mind.[7]
>
> —Apollo Robbins, pickpocket

It's not the tuxedo, it's not the rabbit—a magician's greatest asset is knowing how to control your attention and divert it away from the revealing mechanics of his trick. Using misdirection, he messes with you before your very own eyes, even though you're already suspicious and vigilant. He knows what you think you see, because he is making you think it. How? In *Magic by Midsirection*, Dariel Fitzkee breaks the magician's code of silence to reveal these methods to you, which are detailed below. I'm not suggesting you wear a top hat and start practicing card tricks at a five-year-old's birthday party, but a few of the magician's methods can help you hide, especially when you're under heavy scrutiny.

Frame expectations by setting up some plausible bullshit story. This allows others to think they've come to their own conclusion about what you're up to, while you're actually doing something completely different. "The magician lead[s] the viewer down an explanatory highway from which there is no exit, or, better, from which there are six exits, all of them blocked. . . . He opens a door by pointing to a window."[8] Now, that's some voodoo-sounding shit, right? People like to sound all mysto when they're talking about magicians, but it's simple, useful stuff. If you want to plant malware on Jaycee's computer, don't creep in at the dead of night, dressed like a cat burglar, with all security cameras focused on you. Do it right in the middle of the holiday party. Then act drunk and pop a bunch of balloons while it's downloading. That's magic at work, baby. No one will notice what you're really up to.

INATTENTIONAL (or perceptual) BLINDNESS describes the fact that people can't pay attention to everything in front of them all the time. They will miss very obvious things, especially if they are unexpected.[9] For example, in one study, observers were asked to "count how many times the members of a basketball team passed a ball to one another, while ignoring the passes made by [the other] team. While they concentrated on the counting task, most observers failed to notice a person wearing a gorilla suit walk across the scene [beating his chest]."[10] If you need to get a gorilla out of the building, create a consuming diversion.

Some other useful tips from Mr. Fitzkee: "Movement *attracts* attention but at the same time *reduces* visibility." This is the principle behind all card tricks and sleights of hand. "Naturalness is an anesthetic to attention."[11] When you do what you always do, no one pays attention. You should stick to your routine when you are up to something on the side. As soon as you say, "There's nothing to see here folks," all eyes will be on you.

Many tactics the magician uses are physical versions of those used in arguments. Both magic and arguments use the tools of attention control to distract, or to lead listeners toward a desired conclusion, regardless of whether it's true or not.

IMPLICATION AND SUGGESTION are more effective than direct statements, which run the risk of being disbelieved, especially when you are under suspicion. Start with facts, the truth of which the subject is conclusively aware, then gradually move to things the spectator himself may not personally know to be true. From there, it's easy to jump to the improbable, or even the impossible.

FORESTALL ATTENTION. Take action ahead of time. Do the critical thing before anyone else is alert and concerned about it. If you get caught, remember the ancient Chinese proverb, "It's easier to ask for forgiveness than for permission."

CONFUSE. Mix and blend many and dissimilar details, so it's impossible to distinguish the significant from the insignificant. Disarray and turmoil prevent logical deduction, enabling you to hide the significance of operative details.

DIVERT. Substitute a new, and stronger, interest elsewhere. Magicians often do this by making their functional tools look ordinary and boring—a brown box, a tin can, a table—while the diversion is a hot chick dressed in barely more than a couple of feathers. It's no big stretch to imagine no one's looking at the table. If you want to avoid attracting attention to something, don't look at it or move toward it. If you want to attract attention to a decoy, appear to pay absolute attention to it.

Tip: Never reveal your intentions in advance.

INFORMATION CONTROL

Information control is essential to keep your position secure. Resist letting a secret slip in the name of enthusiasm or bragging. Once a secret is out you can't get it back. This makes the secret useless and potentially damaging. I'm not trying to make you into an exhausted, tight-lipped paranoiac, but it's important to know how to differentiate types of secrets[12] so you be effective at protecting your own, and using other people's as a tool for casual blackmail. Erving Goffman classified six different types of secrets, which are useful for you to know.

DARK SECRET. A secret so hidden, the fact you have a secret is itself hidden. The entire show *Dexter* is about this kind of secret and what happens when people find out about your "dark passenger." The fact that you are a sociopath is a dark secret. It's your core secret, but there are bound to be others. A dark secret is something hidden about you that is antithetical to the way you present yourself to others. Double lives, affairs, moonlighting for another company on the sly, building a spaceship in your garage, are dark secrets. Even if your secret falls far short of something as dramatic as killing hookers at truck stops on the weekend, the secretness itself is what upsets people, so guard them carefully. Discovering your dark secret will cause acute cognitive dissonance in the discoverer, so they will forever distrust and dislike you. Expect an irreparable breach in your relationship, followed by gossip and major damage to your broader professional career. Unless . . . unless your dark secret is something amazing and wonderful, like a masterpiece or a time machine. Or unless you can come up with a humdinger of a redemption story to make your guarding of said secret seem totally understandable and sympathetic. In general, guard dark secrets at all costs.

STRATEGIC SECRET. People know you have it, but don't know the devil in the details. Battle strategies, trade secrets, grandma's pie recipe. If something is "proprietary" or you're forced to sign an NDA, it's a strategic secret. Like the famous secret Coca-Cola recipe. Inside their Atlanta museum, Coke displays a giant flashy safe where the secret is supposedly locked up. But no one knows what the recipe itself is.

Strategic secrets are common in the work environment. And listen to me. No matter how tempting, you must not give these secrets away. Even if they seem small or trivial. You wanna brag at the bar or on Facebook? Save it. The protection of these secrets is much more important to the company than any employee, no matter how great you think they think you are. This is the quickest way to get fired. Do not reveal them, unless you *do* want to get fired and start living large on unemployment benefits. Then, leaking a strategic secret will get the job done quickly and efficiently. As you're getting fired, tell the HR team you will further leak the secret unless they write an acceptable reason for your termination in order to enable you to receive said unemployment benefits. They'll threaten to sue. Tell them they really don't want to have that secret coming up in court. They'll call you an asshole. You'll agree with them. They'll do what you want. And then you'll be home free.

If you want to get a strategic secret out of someone else, hacking, infiltration, and robbery are the most direct means. But that's getting a little melodramatic and movie-plot-ish. Getting people drunk and encouraging people to show you something "real quick" on their phone works better in the real world. Just be alert to the fact that when you're trying to get a secret out of someone else, they may well be trying to get one out of you.

INSIDE SECRET. Think of this kind of secret as knowing about a surprise party or the address of that totally cool after-work drinks spot. Those in the know are separated from everyone else. Inside secrets usually have to do with gossip and social status, and while they may seem frivolous on the surface, they are common currency among those with indirect power. If you find yourself surrounded by people who broker in inside secrets, use it to your advantage. The circulatory system of inside secrets is a great place to spread rumors and gossip, which move quickly, a back channel where you can secretly get other people to blow things up for you.

ENTRUSTED SECRET. A secret shared in confidence. Something you tell your lawyer, as in "I really did kill Nicole." Like the strategic secret, *do not* leak an entrusted secret, no matter how tempting it might be.

FREE SECRET. A secret you can share without getting mud on your face. They are usually offered in a breathless, "I gotta tell you something" or "Did you know" kind of way. These are hardly secrets at all and aren't worth shit. Don't waste your energy guarding free secrets.

LATENT SECRET. These are the ticking time bomb of secrets. All the destructive information is available, but the dots haven't been connected, *yet*. If you're at the center of a damaging latent secret, the best thing you can do is divert attention.

Tip: If you need to take a meeting with someone you suspect is trying to get information out of you, schedule the meeting in an uncomfortable location. In a room with no chairs, groups came to a decision 34 percent faster than in a regular conference room.[13] Remember, when in doubt, it is best to keep it tight. The fewer people in on the secret the better.

CHAPTER 9

LOW-HANGING FRUIT

If you can't spot the sucker in the first half hour at the table, then you are the sucker.

—Mike McDermott, *Rounders*

O nce time has passed and the new-guy phase is over, scrutiny of your movements will naturally be on the wane. Then it's time to start thinking about offense. It's time to have some *fun*. It's time to attack, sow chaos, and cause emotional destruction. The first order of business is to identify easy marks and exploit weak flanks. Here's how.

IMPOSTER SYNDROME

Many people believe they have a job they lucked into or don't deserve. They lack confidence in their abilities, which are usually fine or above average, and are terribly afraid of being exposed. Kind of like that dream where you show up to your high school graduation and then realize you forgot to put on your pants. They fear both failure and success due to their low self-esteem. If you suspect someone might be suffering from imposter syndrome, the first thing to do is decide what you want from them. The answer will lead you to how to best handle exposing them.

They Threaten You and You Want to Get Rid of Them. Shake a paper in their face and speak loudly, with as many people in earshot as possible. Say something like, "What is this supposed to mean? What are you, some kind of fraud?" This will embarrass them and send them skittering for cover. It will also absolutely ruin your chances of having any kind of constructive relationship with them in the future. Ever. Which is good. You don't need this twit.

They Know Something You Want to Learn, Or, You Want Them to Do Something for You. First, boost confidence that their cover is working. Say something like, "You're always so on top of these presentations, Joan, and it's not easy. They're quite complicated." Second, drop a line that presents yourself as someone who feels like they do, but gently, suggesting that it's ridiculous to feel this way. They will be empathetic, but won't lose confidence in you. Say something like, "At my old firm, we used a different program, so sometimes I use screw up the commands here. I know it shouldn't, but it makes me feel like a faker." Third, ask for what you want. "Would you mind looking this over to make sure everything's right before the presentation this afternoon?"

They Threaten Your Path to Promotion, but You Need Them as an Ally. Give her confidence-building affirmations of her work. She'll be grateful and think well of you. At the same time, drop occasional vague doubts about her abilities to everyone else in the office. "Yeah it looks great, but comb through it again just to be sure. I know she means well, but sometimes I wonder if Joan really knows that software as well as she lets on." This will get the others to question her—in her mind: threaten with exposure—which will unnerve and paralyze her, while you come out looking like the good guy.

Someone You Want to Keep in Check. It's useful to keep people back on their heels. Withholding information can make people look stupid and incompetent. Talking casually about other people's failings in an insightful but fun and snarky way can make the imposter-syndrome sufferer worry about the failings you see in them. Work in a little innocent wordplay. Point out things like so-and-so's "baseless promotion" or how Mike really "lucked out." Make a joke about Ms. Winthrop—who clearly lies about her age—as in, "We should make her a 'mock' apple pie for her birthday this year." Phrases like, "Duke's a phony" or little loaded words like *expose, transparent, reveal, lie, fraud,* and *sham* will act like a quick sharp poke in the ribs. In general, consider people's weaknesses as open doors of opportunity for you. When you see an opening, take it.

VANITY

When they're not busy feeling like imposters, people often secretly believe themselves to be greater than they appear to the world.[1] They just haven't been given the proper opportunity to shine. For this reason, flattery is most effective when it reflects how a person wishes to be seen. Excessive or off-the-mark flattery will be seen as false except by the most vain and tends to make people uncomfortable and suspicious. One useful form of flattery is to ask for a favor, sometimes called the Ben Franklin effect. Dale Carnegie cited asking for a favor in *How to Win Friends and Influence People* as "a subtle but effective form of flattery." Another effective form of flattery is agreeing with what people tell you about themselves. It's what they want you to believe and how they want to be perceived. Supporting their claims will make the person feel good, and they will like you for it. Congratulate people on decisions they have made.

ENTRENCHING (THE BACKFIRE EFFECT)

The backfire effect is confirmation bias backed into a corner. The more emotionally charged or deeply held a belief is, the more doggedly a person will hold onto it. Amazingly, contradictory evidence tends to make the original belief stronger. You may think this is the shadowland of the lunatic fringe, conspiracy theories, quack religion, government cover-ups, and Area 54, but even a mundane thing like Obama releasing his birth certificate made some people even more positive he was born in Kenya. This is insane. But again, going back to the strange blindness caused by cognitive bias and belief, it can be most usefully exploited. If you can get someone worked up about a false belief which is advantageous to you, they will hold onto it, no matter what. Get them incensed, and they will swear to you the sky is green. It's dismayingly effective. If you want to obstruct, first get people polarized and feed them antithetical data during stressful situations. Once they start digging in, they will soon be entrenched. Backfire effect is a great way to stoke polarization, but be warned, it is almost impossible to reverse by any rational means, so use it carefully.

Conversely, if you can stay alert to your own irrational belief defenses, if you can force yourself to keep an open mind, you will always have the upper hand.

I know that most men—not only those considered clever, but even those who are very clever, and capable of understanding most difficult scientific, mathematical, or philosophic problems—can very seldom discern even the simplest and most obvious truth if it be such as to oblige them to admit the falsity of conclusions they have formed, perhaps with much difficulty—conclusions of which they are proud, which they have taught to others, and on which they have built their lives.

—Leo Tolstoy, *What Is Art*

ENGINEER LOSSES

Studies in behavioral economics show people hate to lose much more than they love to win.[2] They call it loss aversion. Losing makes people feel really bad. If you want to throw someone off-balance, do what you can covertly to make their projects fail. Think of it as the opposite of insider trading. Withhold important information. Mislead. Stall. Instill doubt.

MANUFACTURE A CRISIS

In the same vein, if your own project looks like it's going to fail, don't just wait for it to happen. Make a big deal out of it. Make it seem like it's more of a disaster than it really is. People will panic, and you will be in an uncomfortable spot—at first. But, when the actual fail occurs, it will be much less serious and people will be relieved. They may even feel that you "saved the day." This may have been what Chicken Little was up to when he ran around yelling "The sky is falling!" Everything after that is greeted with relief.

STOKE FEAR

The more vivid or recent a memory is, the higher the perceived risk associated with that memory. This is known as AVAILABILITY BIAS. For instance, people were more afraid of planes crashing into buildings right after 9/11 than they are now.[3] A good way to increase people's fear of a bad outcome is to remind them of an important or recent incident in which things went horribly

ALBERT

wrong. This will make them nervous. And when they are nervous, they are vulnerable and prone to make mistakes. Even a simple statement like "Well, you remember how *that* went last time," can undermine a person's confidence and put you in charge.

In the 1920s, psychiatrist John B. Watson conducted an experiment that today would probably land him in jail for child abuse, so it's a good thing he got a good one in for science back then. By banging pots and pans whenever the baby boy "Little Albert" was playing with a cute furry thing, over time, Watson was able to make Albert terrified of all sweet furry things. There are subtle ways you can increase a person's reluctance to do something you don't want them to do by linking it psychologically to something unpleasant.

USE THE PULPIT

Fear of public speaking is the most common phobia.[4] Make your underlings stand up in front of everyone else and make presentations whenever possible. They hate it and fear it. It will make them focus on their own anxiety rather than thinking about you. Also in presentation situations, as a speaker, you can use silence to cause anxiety in the audience. Get up there and clear your throat, but say nothing for five to ten seconds. Everyone will get nervous for you. Then say "just kidding" and launch in. Whatever you say after that won't matter.

Silence is a powerful tool in other situations as well, because it makes people so uncomfortable. Cops and trial lawyers use prolonged silences to get suspects to blurt out secrets just to fill up the dead air. Angry spouses use silence to break each other. A great way of drawing the other guy out is to ask people to talk about themselves, then listen. Two things will happen: 1) You'll learn things that may be useful later if a little coercion is required; 2) They'll probably like you because you seem so interested in them.

LET THEM SELF-DESTRUCT IN A PUBLIC WAY

Incompetent people "fail to recognize their own lack of skill, grossly overesti-mate their abilities and are unable to recognize talent in other people."[5] This is Jimmy. He sits two seats to your left and has a boomy voice that lands hard on the "d's", which he uses to crow boldly on every fucking phone, calling atten-tion to the fact that he has no clue about anything. He's also an arrogant prick running in your lane. You daydream of crushing him with a front loader. But hold on a minute. This is a perfect scenario where you should relax. Instead of trying to shut him down, encourage his boldness, leave his mistakes in full view and convince him to bring his worst ideas forward. In short, as the old saying goes, "Give him enough rope to hang himself."

HARNESS THE POWER OF THE HERD

While you understand rules are at core "created for someone else's comfort and peace of mind,"[6] most people don't appreciate this fact. They accept rules as real, as in actual things like guardrails or drawbridges. They believe the empty tautology "rules are rules" actually means something. This makes some self-preservation sense when breaking rules is met with punishment. But the psy-chological acceptance of following the rules extends far beyond obedience. It taps into the core desire of many to fit in with the majority and to follow the status quo. Studies show that 76 percent of people will agree with a group's unanimous (and visibly, empirically false) decision so as not to appear stupid, even if they can see the herd answer is clearly wrong.[7] Harness this power of social consensus. Everyone wants to fit in.

STATUS QUO Status quo bias is a fancy name for inertia. Behavioral economist Richard Thaler says, "Never underestimate the power of inertia."[8] People stay in terrible relationships and dead-end jobs they hate out of inertia. The good thing for you about inertia is that when people are doing what they've always done, they're less likely to be paying careful attention to anything. They are not on guard. They are not scrutinizing. This give you greater latitude to operate on the sly. If you want to promote somnambulant behavior, don't change anything.

On the other hand, if you want to agitate someone or direct someone's attention away from what you're up to, upend their inertia. This is easy to do. Make new rules for the parking lot. Change the network operating systems. Introduce a new, mandatory, and confusing piece of software. Move the break room to another floor. It's amazing how worked up people will get without realizing that what's upsetting them is change itself, not the stupid thing you are changing.

Related to this is something Thaler calls CHOICE ARCHITECTURE. This simply means that people will choose things they perceive to be the easiest and most direct, so the manner in which you present their options affects their choice. If you don't want someone to choose "A," put obstacles in front of it. This can be something as simple as requiring an obnoxiously complicated password every time they try to access "A." Conversely, make what you want them to choose seem easy and direct, even if it's less advantageous to them in real terms.

TRUE CONFESSIONS

"People hide behind laws and customs and society and hierarchy because they are a bunch of chickenshits."

—Judith Smalley, bartender. Denver, Colorado.

BULLYING

This should not be your first choice of action when dealing with someone you cannot control. It is messy, public, and the results aren't exactly foolproof. However, if you find yourself in a really tight spot, you should know that at least 25 percent of people bullied at the workplace quit their jobs.[9] So keep bullying in your back pocket.

MONEY DOESN'T TALK, IT SWEARS

It is difficult to get a man to understand something, when his salary depends on his not understanding it.
—Upton Sinclair *I, Candidate for Governor: And How I Got Licked*[10]

This one is fun. If you really want to shake someone from the tree, find out how much more money their colleague earns, then let the person making less know the difference. You will instantly spark a deep unrest and resentment. Frans de Waal's famous study on pay inequality in monkeys illustrates this to hilarious effect. (You can watch it here: https://www.youtube.com/watch?v=meiU6TxysCg.) This will shake up the department and no one will blame you for causing trouble because they will be focusing all their ire on their cheating backstabbing boss.

There are all sorts of inventive ways to identify and exploit weakness. Encourage worry and self-destruction whenever possible without drawing attention to yourself. Pick off the easy ones first, they are good practice. You'll need it.

CHAPTER 10

ALLIES

Samuel Stote: What's a misanthrope, Arthur?

Two Bob: Some bugger who fuckin' hates every other bugger.

Arthur Burns: He's right Samuel. A misanthrope is one who hates humanity.

Samuel Stote: Is that what we are, misanthropes?

Arthur Burns: Good lord no. We're a family.

—Nick Cave, *The Proposition*

You've infiltrated the institution and are doing fine. Your job and your ladder to success have been secured. You've spent a lot of time on hiding your true nature, but there are occasions when your sociopathic traits can make you popular. This is a short chapter because, let's face it, you're never going to be a "people" person. That said, here are a few good ways to get allies, because you might need them at times.

SPILLOVER

Chickenshit people like to draft behind those who are willing to take most of the blame and leave spoils to those riding in their wake. While many of your inherent traits can be seen as dangerous, irresponsible, and threatening to superiors, to your peers they can provide a lot of exciting cover, which leads to loyalty. This is the deep truth known by Mob bosses, corrupt politicians, and the like. Known as "the spillover effect,"[1] it can be both useful and fun.

In his article "Why It Pays to Be a Jerk," writer Jerry Useem writes: "Spend some time with the [jerks] of the world and you're apt to get things you are not entitled to. . . . Life seemed larger, grander—like the world was a little more at your feet—when they were around."[2] This is where you can let loose. People sometimes "want the excitement, the dangerous mayhem that psychopaths can offer,"[3] as long as they are protected from the consequences and get a share of the spoils: the spillover. Everyone loved the Wolf of Wall Street while he was shedding money on them. Encourage others to pad their expense accounts, while you provide cover if anything untoward comes to light. "Don't worry, I'll take care of it" is something you aren't afraid to say, and that's rare. It allows the more cautious and nervous others to participate in an illicit thrill while you simultaneously absorb their fear. You can take care of it because you have that amazing ability to stay cool while lying through your teeth. Unencumbered by social anxieties, fear of being found out, empathy, remorse, or guilt, you can give your team excitement, protection, and spillover benefits they would normally be too scared to collect for themselves. It's a way to make allies through vicarious thrill. Some people like to be friends with assholes, and don't even think about the fact you would throw them to the dogs if need be. Spillover is like the fun cousin of corruption. It requires less power, is not necessarily illegal, and is wonderfully obnoxious.

> He was an exciting guy. He was really nice. He introduced me to everybody. Everybody wanted to be nice to him. And he knew how to handle it.
>
> —Karen, *Goodfellas*

Here's another example. Carter was working on a film with an unreasonably cheap and unpleasant production manager who had to approve all expenditures. Carter wanted twelve lights. The production manager said she'd only pay for six. In response, Carter told his crew "she's gonna pay the asshole tax" and after the shoot he let his guys break some of the lights so the damage cost equalled the amount of the original twelve-light rental request. This made Carter a hero for getting one over on the production manager, who everyone hated. She had a fit but couldn't prove anything. Carter enjoyed tremendous goodwill from everyone else for the rest of the shoot.

Tip: When you get in hot water and can't lie your way out of it, minimize the outlandishness of your behavior. Trivialize the situation, understate your role, and remember you can always say, "I was just joking."

Here are some other popular characters you can play with your sociopathic strengths:

THE JACKASS. There is no bigger vicarious thrill than seeing Johnny Knoxville get rammed in the nuts by an angry bull. Why? Because he's fucking laughing. If you're willing to do things other people are too scared to do and enjoy it, you will always have fans.

THE FIXER. A person in corrupt or war-torn locales who gets people, reporters, supplies, or anything else, in and out of dangerous places and difficult situations is a fixer. If you can use your fearlessness and calm under pressure to provide cover for someone else, they will revere you. Everyone is grateful for a fixer.

THE WISEASS. Another vicarious thrill some people enjoy is when you're willing to say the things you know they're thinking but are too rude for them to say themselves. If you're rude first, it paves the way for others. You're the icebreaker. Being a wiseass is greatly assisted by your being funny.

That's the kind of Porsche that dentists drive.
—Steve Jobs, about a lower-end Porsche in the Apple parking lot[4]

Remember this: people are often drawn to transgression and spoils as long as they don't feel in danger themselves.

TRUE CONFESSIONS
"Mostly, I would say, I have a flexible conscience."
—Moses Chambers, musician. Los Angeles, California.

CREATE TITLES AND AWARDS

If you don't feel like playing the badass, there are other simple ways to manipulate people into liking you. Once you are in a position of power, creating titles and awards is an inexpensive way to make people happy and proud. And they will like you for it. Michael Korda notes: "The organization has an interest in encouraging the natural propensity of men and women toward self-aggrandizement, if only by means of symbolic awards."[5] Company picnics. Medals and awards. Gold watches. Swag (a.k.a. participation trophies for adults). Constant title inflation is another symptom of this steady desire for self-aggrandizement. It's a cheap and effective psychic bread and circus, and you should use it.

In the fifties, companies started handing out the VP title with abandon. Nowadays, look at the scrawl on a movie and you might see as many as twenty credited producers where there used to be one. Fifty years ago, Twiggy the superthin supermodel wore a size eight. That same size today is called a double zero. Marilyn Monroe's size twelve in the 1960s would today be a size six.[6] As people got fatter, the clothiers just made the sizes bigger, so everyone could keep feeling good about themselves. There's a steady march of feelings over facts, and people are suckers for it. Stroke their egos and put their weaknesses to work for you.

CHAPTER 11

PRESSURE

Never apologize, never explain. Get it over with and let them howl.

—Benjamin Jowett

Now that the easy pickings are out of the way, you have graver concerns ahead. In any job worth having, serious people will inevitably put pressure on you. You should treat it as a compliment.

HOW TO REACT WHEN UNDER ATTACK

People are used to you. You know what you need to do. You've worked hard on your affable vanilla character. You've pegged your office mates' operational styles, so you have an effective shorthand helping you breeze through the everyday scuffles as they crop up. You've figured out how to minimize cognitive dissonance, control information, and present yourself with expressive coherence. And it's working. Sure, you've slipped up a few times. A little fraud. A bribe or two. It's so easy. Disappeared some emails. Slipped Mrs. Jansen's lost ring in your pocket. . . . But you are unburdened by care. This can be a weakness.

You're becoming enmeshed in the office culture and developing a history. It can't be helped. While irritating, in order to make your manipulations successful, you need to take the long view and pay extra attention to planning. You're not a planner by nature, but one thing you must plan for is what to do when you get caught. Sooner or later someone is going to get wise to you. Two things can happen. One, someone will find out something shady that you did, or two, they will develop the sense that you're hiding something. While they won't necessarily know you're hiding the fact that you are a sociopath, both of these problems will require heavier defense than your faux vanilla self.

> You don't even walk like a normal person, you glide like a fuckin lizard on ice . . . It's all a fuckin act and I ain't buying it.
>
> —James Doakes, *Dexter*

TRUE CHARACTER. Robert McKee, seminar self-help guru for wannabe screenwriters says "true character is revealed in the choices a human being makes under pressure—the greater the pressure, the deeper the revelation, the truer the choice to the character's essential nature."[1] If someone's putting the screw to you, it's time to let go of your vanilla character. He can't help you now. You need to have a heroic backstory ready to deploy to your boss when the chips are down. You need something a little flashier, a little more complicated, a character who can be forgiven for the newly discovered transgression.

The good news is people are suckers for certain kinds of character weaknesses. They love fatal flaws.[2] They love redemption stories and vulnerability stories.

Presidential candidate Ben Carson enjoyed a surge in ratings after he confessed to having attempted to stab a family member as a youth but later changed his ways, seeking God's grace and redemption. Nice screenplay. Of course, neither the seeking nor the stabbing (supposedly stopped by a belt buckle) were verified, but the story made people feel he was sympathetic . . . and a badass. People eat up this kind of shit. In his case, Ben used a literal sin and a redemption-by-God type scenario to please evangelicals specifically, but this is not what I am promoting. This example is intended to illustrate how stories that admit a weakness, matched with an attempt to see it fixed, can elicit magnanimous and generous feelings.

Craft a redemptive life story. Just make one up. It should relate to something you are most likely to get in trouble for, and you should keep it a secret until you are cornered and in need. A sympathy story is most powerful the first time it's told. Its key ingredient is shame. An amazing nonverbal example of this came from Victorian England: poor women rented healthy babies to go beg with. The mother got a free babysitter and the beggar got an irresistible prop to go along with the immediately "apparent" redemption story, "I am the most wretched among wretches, a poor single mother, but no matter my transgressions I will stop at nothing to care for this innocent lamb. Look how healthy she is compared to me. Give her a shilling."

If a redemptive story seems just too phony for you to tell convincingly, other narratives can help shore up questionable behavior. Present yourself as an underdog who has faced down a tremendous challenge in your past (e.g., the gross jobs you had to do to put yourself through college) or about a time you fell short, but learned a lesson (e.g., I took a little change out of the till, and even though I never did it again sometimes all the fear comes back to me). You can connect with others by describing your past in a way your questioner may relate to (When I was on the football team . . . you remember football . . . the beer, the girls . . . right?). There are plenty of other options. In fact, the storyline behind almost any heartwarming movie plot should do the trick. Presenting a vulnerability will likely result in a lighter punishment than you deserve.

If these tactics don't work, you can always resort to stonewalling. Just keep quiet and don't give them anything they can use against you. *When in doubt, don't tell people anything.*

BULLSHIT

Bullshit is a statement "unconstrained by a concern for the truth" says philosopher Harry G. Frankfurt.[3] And he is right. Not quite the same as lying, bullshit is a way to get out of something without needing to either deceive, win, or prove anything. The goal is to simply get past something as quickly as possible with a minimal amount of damage, and no quotable assertions. Bullshit is "unavoidable whenever circumstances require someone to talk without knowing what he is talking about." Partly for this reason, Frankfurt believes people "tend to be more tolerant of bullshit than of lies, perhaps because we are less inclined to take the former as a personal affront." He insightfully quotes Eric Ambler's *Dirty Story*: "Never tell a lie when you can bullshit your way through." This is good advice under pressure.

If you can't dazzle them with brilliance, baffle them with bullshit.

—W. C. Fields

EMPTY SPEAK is a simple form of bullshit: saying something without really meaning anything. For example, the popular response "It is what it is." Use overbroad terms that can apply to just about any situation, and which are in line with what people are already inclined to believe. This is a great time to exploit bias. When Henry comes in with some mixed sales reviews and asks, "Are we going to need to cut the Janks model from our productions line?" You say, "It's going to be a great year for you, Henry." (Optimism bias at work). Then pat him on the shoulder, check your phone, and hurry off.

Astrology is a good example of soothing empty verbiage that encourages belief. Practice speaking the way people write astrology and your bullshitting ability will improve. Astrological forecasts are skillfully written to support bias without clouding the picture with concrete details; they are wonderful primers on how to write in an appealing, nearly content-free manner. Everybody half-believes them, because they always contain a kernel of something everybody wants to believe about themselves. Empty speak is one way to breeze past an answer you don't know. Keep it positive. The Magic 8 Ball has been a beloved toy for the past seventy years. The answers are vague, yet appealing. This long-term popularity may be due to the fact that the 8 Ball contains ten positive answers, while only five noncommittal and five negative ones.

NONSENSE is another way.

All you have to do is say something nobody understands and they'll do practically anything you want them to.

—J. D. Salinger, *The Catcher in the Rye*

There's all sorts of nonsense out there in the world. If you're an expert with a handle on big words, you can spout off an impossible yet complex-sounding procedure required before you can finish the task at hand. We might call this shoptalk nonsense. It's very effective, especially if you can make it seem ever so subtly off-putting as well. If you're getting pressure because a job's not finished offer to show your manager why: "The current oscillator is askew, so each individual induction wire will need to be recalibrated before I can continue . . . why don't you come down to the basement and I can show you. I think we got the last of the rats down there yesterday." It's a lot like empty speak, but is full of sham specifics.

WORD SALAD is another popular form of nonsense. Originally coined to describe the garbled nonsensical way schizophrenics sometimes talk, it's now used to describe a popular form of bullshit. Word salad can be used tactically to derail someone asking difficult questions without your painting yourself into a truth corner. Choose a few descriptive and colorful words from the question posed and add some power words like *because, therefore,* or *in response.* The result will likely qualify as an answer, if confusing, and you will not be held accountable to the facts of an outright lie.

Here's an example by Donald Trump during one of his campaign stops. It's a little long, but amazing:

> Look, having nuclear—my uncle was a great professor and scientist and engineer, Dr. John Trump at MIT; good genes, very good genes, OK, very smart, the Wharton School of Finance, very good, very smart— you know, if you're a conservative Republican, if I were a liberal, if, like, OK, if I ran as a liberal Democrat, they would say I'm one of the smartest people anywhere in the world—it's true!—but when you're a conservative Republican they try—oh, do they do a number—that's why I always start off: Went to Wharton, was a good student, went there, went there, did this, built a fortune—you know I have to give my like credentials all the time, because we're a little disadvantaged—but you look at the nuclear deal, the thing that really bothers me—it would have been so easy, and it's not as important as these lives are (nuclear is powerful; my uncle explained that to me many, many years ago, the power and that was thirty-five years ago; he would explain the power of what's going to happen and he was right—who would have thought?), but when you look at what's going on with the four prisoners—now

it used to be three, now it's four—but when it was three and even now, I would have said it's all in the messenger; fellas, and it is fellas because, you know, they don't, they haven't figured that the women are smarter right now than the men, so, you know, it's gonna take them about another hundred-and-fifty years—but the Persians are great negotiators, the Iranians are great negotiators, so, and they, they just killed, they just killed us.[4]

The questioner will be flummoxed, if not convinced. While not exactly a win, it will buy you some time. A more powerful use of word saladism is to invert the meaning of a statement or question by simply transposing the words offered. For example:

"Because it's better to die on one's feet than live on one's knees . . ."
"I'm afraid you have it backward. It is better to *live* on one's feet than die on one's knees. *That* is the way the saying goes."

—Joseph Heller, *Catch* 22

This is more like a "meaning salad" with meat. If you can come up with one, your interlocutor will be surprised, confused, and maybe even driven to deep thought. Advantage: sociopath.

THE ARTFUL DODGER. Unpredictable patterns and a lack of feedback are great ways to undermine a person's sense of control, which is why you should never tell anyone the real reason you did something, unless it's useful to do so.[5] Use wicked turns of phrase to deflect even the most pointed questions. Bluff. Answer a question with a question. Try broad "black hole" questions like, "What's the downside of doing nothing?" or "Can you explain that again?" Learn the power of throwing the old "What Jack says about Jill, says more about Jack than about Jill" in your interlocutor's face. Always remember to dissemble; disguise your motives and your feelings.

Tip: As shown with cognitive dissonance, people are thrown off-balance when things don't make sense. Use this to your advantage by throwing "verbal dissonance" back at a questioning attacker. When someone is peeling back your mask, throw mixed metaphors at them. The time required to figure out what you actually mean and the ensuing confusion—because it sounds so familiar yet makes no sense—will make them stumble. With an affable smile, try saying something like "Don't cry wolf over spilled milk" or "Why kick a gift horse in the teeth?"

Hedge, invent words, make contradictory assertions. Leave the impression of having had a good talk, while keeping it content-free.

Modern Drunkard offers good advice on acing an intervention that can be effective in dodging just about every difficult situation. They suggest you "muster all your inner strength and screw an indulgent and reasonable smile onto your face" and shine a favorable light on your questionable behavior:

"'Frank, I watched you drink a whole bottle of cheap vodka!'

'It was all I could afford. Surely you don't want me blowing my paycheck on some imported brand.'"[6]

EQUIVOCATING. This form of stalling is useful when you need to reply but all definite answers open to you seem like bad ones. Respond in a vague, noncommittal way while trying to alter the line of questioning. Some call it tap dancing. President Clinton presented one of the most famous equivocal answers during his grand jury testimony. "It depends on what the meaning of the word 'is' is." A sophisticated form of bullshit.

LYING

> [Politicians] never rise beyond the level of misrepresentation, and actually condescend to prove, to discuss, to argue. How different from the temper of the true liar, with his frank, fearless statements, his superb irresponsibility, his healthy, natural disdain of proof of any kind!
>
> —Oscar Wilde, "The Decay of Lying"

Lying is something broadly practiced. Oliver James asserts that one in five communications contains a white lie. "Many lies are said to protect others' feelings but some are necessary and healthy deceptions that advance our inter-ests."[7] You should feel free to use white lies, but they're not what we're talking about here. Instead, let's discuss three other kinds of lying which, according to the former CIA interrogation officers behind the book *Spy the Lie* are cov-ered by the oath "the truth" (explicit lies) "the whole truth" (implicit lies) "and nothing but the truth" (lies of influence).

Implicit lies use omission and distraction to create a false impression without asserting something provably untrue. Our sage Goffman advises that when challenged, "appear to answer the question completely with statements that can be proved accurate, yet disclose really nothing."[8] As with bullshit, people tend to be less offended by implicit lies than by ones which can be proven brazenly false. The point being to alter the other's perception of what's going on, while not providing false information. This is the essence of the implicit lie. But it is easier said than done, my friend. Which is why you, the sociopath should just go for the explicit, bald-faced lie. People don't expect this kind of brazen lying because you can get caught totally red-handed, which makes most people too nervous to try it.

Explicit lies are more assertive and influential, but also more dangerous; you claim something which is not true, that did not happen, you were not there. The problem with these lies is should they be exposed, you will face dire conse-quences. They make people very angry. But if you feel your current situation has become untenable without lying, float one out there. You may get fired for it, but at least it won't be today. It's worth noting, the more outrageous the lie, the less likely someone is going to disbelieve it, because they can't believe you would actually tell such a whopper. So if you have to lie outright, go big.

Lies of influence occur when people couch their answer in a broader posi-tive description of themselves, as in "How can you even ask me if I took the cookies, I'm a Girl Scout troop leader!" According to the CIA experts, lies of influence are very effective. So use them. Be a little incredulous. Say "I would never do that . . . it would be dishonest." Professional lie detectors will smell a rat, but most people will be swayed by the weight of your upright moral character.

Whichever kind of lie, if you do find telling one to be necessary, do it well. A few ways these CIA experts detect lies can inform you how to lie better, though they would vehemently deny this. So let me both paraphrase and subvert at the same time. First, humans are disinclined to lie outright. When asked "Did you do it?" people will try to avoid saying "No" directly. As a sociopath, you do not suffer this same discomfort, so use it to your advantage. Just do it. Do not hesitate. Say no. Don't try to mitigate the denial with qualifiers like "I didn't do nothing to nobody" or "Basically" or "To be perfectly honest." Don't offer a rambling, long-winded answer. Do not repeat the question; it will be seen as an attempt to buy time. Do not remain silent. Do not respond with a nonanswer like, "Now that's an interesting question." Do not attack your accuser with something like, "Are you even a real police officer?" Do not get overly specific as in "I was not at the 7-Eleven at 5:36 p.m. on April fourteenth." Don't get overly polite all of a sudden. Don't say "No, sir" if you don't usually say "sir." Don't "swear to Christ" or other such nonsense. Don't get indignant. Do not pretend you don't understand the question.[9] An immediate, firm, and calm "No" is your best strategy. "I don't remember" can provide a dubious stalling tactic if you're in a pinch, but you're bigger than that.

Our professional CIA lie detectors say that "at least two-thirds of our communication is accomplished nonverbally."[10] So, as previously discussed, mind your body language. Don't nod your head while saying no. Don't cover your mouth or eyes when answering. Don't stutter with your body: no throat clearing, licking lips, swallowing, shifting your weight, etc. Stay cool! Also, according to pronoun expert Pennebaker "I is used at far higher rates by followers than by leaders, truth tellers than liars"[11] so for once, use "I" a lot when lying.

Practice makes perfect. You can become better at lying, so work on it. You never know when you will really need this skill. As Thomas Jefferson said, "He who permits himself to tell a lie once, finds it much easier to do it a second and third time, till at length it becomes habitual." Just remember, outright lying requires focus and follow-through. It's a pain in the ass, and has to be remembered down to the last detail.

At the same time, you don't want to go too big or make your lie too interesting. Know when to temper your lies. Con man Christian Gerhartsreiter was long believed to be Clark Rockefeller. And because he didn't claim he was from *the* Rockefellers, no one bothered to check up on him. As journalist Mark Seal noted: "He intimated that he was from the Percy Rockefeller branch of the clan—not John D. ultra\rich, but plenty rich."[12] He had learned his lesson.

Earlier in his career—as Christopher Crowe—he'd disastrously used serial killer David Berkowitz's (Son of Sam) social security number as his own and was busted in short order. Why did he do it? No idea. Totally pointless. Not a winning sociopathic move. Don't do this kind of shit. Don't be tempted into telling lies you think are cool or clever but that could draw scrutiny. Pick something a little less direct. Like being a Rockefeller, but not "the" Rockefeller. It can still be pretty obvious, just not *that* obvious. Clever author Dale Carnegie changed his last name from Carnegey to match the spelling of the illustrious steel magnate, but never claimed to be directly related. He let people assume.

APPLYING PRESSURE

In addition to deflecting pressure, if you want to get anywhere in life, it's essential to know how to apply pressure effectively.

DEADLINES. Time pressure has long been seen as an effective management tool to encourage task completion. Not surprisingly, deadlines are widely employed to "get 'er done." But what you should focus on is the fact that unrealistic deadlines can be used to make things fall apart. If you want to force a fail, set an impossible deadline. This will put people into panic mode and let you go about your business without scrutiny. Standing over someone and sweating them is also an effective means of forcing mistakes. Always remember what security company president Gavin de Becker said: "When you remove time . . . you are subject to the lowest-quality intuitive reaction . . . I think that we become temporarily autistic also in situations when we run out of time."[13]

MOVE THE GOALPOST. Even when someone meets your expectation, have another demand ready. Never let anything be considered complete. Leave loose ends and unfinished business. Most people yearn for closure but you don't care. Leave it open. It's no bother to you and will drive others crazy. Constant rumination and permanent provocations make people edgy.

ARGUMENTS

Water runs uphill . . . toward money.

—Water "law" of Los Angeles ca. 1900

At some point, arguments are about winning. Sure, there are those which endeavor to get at "the truth," but usually arguments are either about getting your way or convincing an undecided party that you are right. Once you get to the argument phase, both sides are probably pretty entrenched with their biases operating in overdrive, so facts aren't going to work. If getting at the truth is essential to getting your way, it is best to present your facts in a non-confrontational, private setting where your opponent has the chance to calmly absorb the new information without feeling like he is "losing face." If this doesn't work and the discussion escalates into a full-blown argument, fuck it. Make sure others can hear you and say anything to win. Many of these tactics are used by lawyers and politicians to great effect. Remember that winning an argument has little to do with being right.

> Forget facts. People think emotionally. Intuitions mostly dictate what is right or wrong. People usually conclude first, then pull out resources to support their beliefs. This is why using narratives and analogies, etc., is much more effective than actual facts when giving a speech or making an argument. People are also more likely to remember stories over numbers, statistics, etc. So, don't get hung up on factual accuracy.
>
> —Laura Avery, lawyer, New Orleans

Here's a real example of how astonishingly ineffective it can be to deploy facts—even a basic proven empirical fact—against someone hell-bent on a particular argument:

G: Won't it be great when you get back? It'll be daylight savings time and we'll have an extra hour of daylight.
A: It won't be an extra hour, just a different part of the day when the sun is up.

G: No. See when you get back, we'll have changed the clocks and will get an extra hour of light. During daylight savings we get more sunlight.
A: Changing the clocks doesn't change how the earth orbits the sun, it just changes what time we say it is.
G: No. It gives us an extra hour of daylight!

As with everything else, confidence is essential to winning arguments. A baseless contradiction asserted with confidence can be quite effective. Here are some other ways to get the win during an argument. We'll start nice and go to nasty. Advice for you: when in doubt, escalate. Once you are at the heated-argument phase, winning is the only way to go.

The first line of attack is to deflect, confuse, frustrate, or derail the other person's argument.

LEVEL 1: ASK QUESTIONS AND INSTILL DOUBT

When you find yourself mired and on the defensive during a complex argument, one solid course of action is to undermine the other's sense of being "armed with the facts." Initiate doubt, change the subject, tap dance, and answer a question with a question.

ASK FOR AN EXPLANATION. Ask why someone holds a certain opinion or belief. Stay quiet and let them try to explain. They may well find they have no idea, and are simply parroting what the morning paper or their cronies in legal said last week. In extreme cases, they may even shake their own belief for themselves. (More likely, they will play back with you and send up a diversionary flare, hoping you will take the bait. Pay no attention.) A more aggressive form of this: make a claim—true, false, whatever—then challenge your opponent to disprove it.

Another effective tactic to minimize the brunt of the argument and defend against prying questions is to introduce general expansive questions like, "That may be true but isn't it also true that . . . ?" Use "What ifs?" to open the line of questioning and create an environment of curiosity, rather than direct attack.

Similarly, "Would it be helpful if" can be an effective way to shift focus from problems to solutions—which should be your solutions.

INTRODUCE DOUBT. Ask "Are you certain? Are you positive? Are you sure?" Most people are hesitant to answer a definitive question because at root, no, we aren't sure of anything. For hundreds of years philosophers have been trying (and failing) to disprove the idea that we can't even prove we exist. We can't even prove that we're not just brains in vats being manipulated by scientist aliens to believe we are experiencing so-called reality. But enough about that. Once a person hesitates, doubt is introduced. Doubt is the antidote to confidence and it erodes an opinion, as effectively as confidence bolsters one. Doubt is not contradictory information but rather pure, fact-free uncertainty. If you can get someone to doubt their own assertion, the argument is nearly won.

LEVEL 2: DISTRACT AND CONFUSE

You can win by diverting the discussion away from the main point of your argument toward matters that will be more readily accepted, even (or especially) if they have nothing to do with the matter at hand. Distraction is your biggest ally in arguments you are not winning. If you can exasperate the other into sputtering silence or incoherent rage, even better. You win. Even though your original point has never been accepted or agreed to, it will live to face another day.

Example: If you find yourself in a rancorous argument over a two-state solution between Israel and Palestine, lead the conversation toward water rights and pretty soon, if you are skilled enough, you can get the other guy to spout off about how broccoli is better than cauliflower. This is one way of winning an argument. It's called changing the subject.

Use rhetorical tricks to lead the argument away from the core topic, so it becomes irrelevant and there is no way for you to lose. Change the subject often. Turn the argument into a farce. If someone cites an example that took place in Ohio, start talking about Ohio. Even something as obvious as "Oh, my step-aunt was from Ohio" can effectively divert an argument. In his skits, comedian Chevy Chase used to create escapes from awkward situations by doing things like intentionally spilling red wine all over himself, falling down the stairs, or knocking over a Christmas tree. Especially when on defense, distraction is everything. Shift ground. Ignore the point.

LEVEL 3: WEAR DOWN

REPEAT YOURSELF SICK. As we've seen, measured repetition can promote belief. But by this stage in an argument there's no time left for changing belief. Even so, repetition can be used in a different way: as a bludgeon. If your opponent refutes an assertion, repeat it. Increase the frequency of your repetition. Repeat it into the ground. Exasperate them. Make them sick to death of fucking hearing it over and over and over and over. First, they'll sigh. Then, they'll puke. Then, they'll give up. This will take stamina and willpower on your part because you also will want to kill yourself if you have to hear it one more time. But stick with it and you'll get your way—even if they still won't "believe" you—they'll agree just to get you to shut up. A good indicator of when you've won in this manner is when someone says, "OK OK OK OK OK OK OK, Jesus. OK!"

DOUBLE NEGATIVES. These are inherently confusing and can be used to exhaust and irritate your opponent. Simply phrasing something with a double negative can make it seem more convoluted than it actually is. Ask things like, "Is it not not true that anyone ate none of the doughnuts I bought you guys?"

LEVEL 4: DIG AND PROD

GENERALIZE THROUGH STORYTELLING. A memorable anecdote can effectively bolster a wider claim. Start with a powerful single instance and generalize from there. The force and specificity of the telling will resonate with the listener and make it seem like if it could happen once, it could happen a thousand times. "Well, look at Jordan Bills—he was shot dead in the street last year for nothing more than jaywalking. How can you say jaywalking isn't dangerous?"

POKE HOLES. Find fault in your opponent's reasoning, then claim his mistake proves his conclusion is wrong, even if the error has nothing to do with the conclusion's validity. Put a hyperfocus on this one irrelevant fact or wrong assertion and ignore everything else. In this way, you can amplify mistakes to gain leverage.

PROBABLY TRUE IS TRUE. If something may possibly be the case and it's to your advantage, assume it is true. Proceed from there and make your opponent waste his energy on attempting to prove that it is false.

MISQUOTE. Take a snippet of your opponent's speech out of context and intentionally misunderstand it. Put words in their mouth. Depict them as having an outlandish viewpoint they don't possess. This will also make them angry, which leads us to . . .

LEVEL 5: INFURIATE

A more strident line of attack is to focus solely on making your opponent lose their cool. This argument style will drive your opponent crazy, and you don't need to rely on facts. Use fun, creative zingers, to irritate your opponent; they are irrefutable because they make no sense. Remember, whoever loses their temper loses the argument. Your goal here is to be confusing and frustrating. If someone gasps, "You're impossible!" or pretends to choke themselves, you've won.

CIRCULAR ARGUMENTS. Arguments where the premise and conclusion are the same assertion are guaranteed to exasperate your opponent.

"We're all mad here. I'm mad. You're mad."

"How do you know I'm mad?" said Alice.

"You must be," said the Cat, "or you wouldn't have come here."

—Lewis Carroll, *Alice in Wonderland*

LOADED QUESTIONS. Ask a question that contains a nasty presumption. The most famous example comes from *Clear Thinking* by R. W. Jepson: "Have you ceased beating your wife?" How do you even begin to answer that?

CATCH-22. A paradoxical logical trap, where the rules contradict themselves, and there is no way to escape. People find these infuriating and associate them with Kafka, bureaucracies, and, of course, the book that made them famous, *Catch-22.* One common example deals with unions: you can't join the union unless you've worked a union job and you can't work a union job unless you are already in the union. Here's the core example from *Catch-22*: "Orr was crazy and could be grounded. All he had to do was ask; and as soon as he did, he would no longer be crazy and would have to fly more missions. . . . Anyone who wants to get out of combat duty isn't really crazy."

LEVEL 6: ATTACK

Once you are slinging vitriol, this is no longer an argument, this is a fight. The more out-there the attack, the more uproarious the result. Some call these tactics below the belt but in a street fight, kicking someone in the balls can keep you from getting stabbed in the belly and you are here to establish dominance and to win, no matter what.

BE DISMISSIVE. Call someone's argument absurd or "stone-cold crazy." Be incredulous, as in, "How could you possibly believe the earth is round? That's patently absurd!" This style is sometimes known as *argumentum ad lapidem* or "appeal to the stone."

DISPARAGE. "There's a difference between skepticism and disparagement" said James Clapper, former director of national intelligence. And indeed there is. Skepticism only calls into question the veracity of a claim. Disparagement does two things at once; it calls the claim's veracity into question *and* questions the honesty of the person making the claim. It's sort of like throwing a skunk at an attacking dog. It's economical, a heavy lifter which can be used to violently deflect your opponent's argument. Be warned however, it is also seen as harsh and can make people angry. Its power lies in conflating dissenting voices with dishonesty.

SAVAGE. Insult their intelligence. Call them names. Employ an ad hominem attack, which American theorist Stuart Chase characterized as one "where the issue is deserted to attack the character of the person who raises it."[14] A famous ad hominem attack from the 2016 presidential debates was Trump calling Clinton "such a nasty woman." No one remembers what they were arguing about, but everyone remembers that line. It was effective. The stronger will win and the "truth" will be nowhere to be seen. The problem is, once both sides are savaging each other in the gutter, where do you go from there? It's a difficult position to back away from. On that note, a wise piece of advice from Robert Greene from his book *The Art of Seduction*: "It is particularly important to avoid insulting those in a position to injure you."

TACTICAL THREATS. Studies show a cool, viable threat, such as "take the deal or I walk," is both more effective and generates less ill will than does an angry threat.[15] This is especially true when the threat is issued fairly late in the negotiation game, when it is less likely to be seen as empty. So hold off. Wait to deliver your threat until your opponent is deeply engaged. At that time, a quiet threat can effectively break a heated exchange while making you look calm and in control.

THREATS OF INJURY. Scare tactics are more complicated. They definitely attract attention, but also foster resistance and anger. Consider threats of violence, firings, etc., as a mixed bag similar to bullying. They can be effective in certain situations but expect the blowback to be fierce. If you must use it, remember that fear generally works better to stop people doing things than to make them do something.[16] You have far better tricks. Besides, once a person fears you, they are more likely to pay closer attention to your every move.

THE SELL

Salesmen excel at applying pressure. They make you want what they are selling, and make you believe it's worth the price they are asking. They do this by telling an appealing fairytale about: 1) Who you will "be" when you own this product (think luxury goods); 2) How sad you will be if you miss the opportunity to have this amazing product (for a limited time only!); 3) How valuable the product is and why you are getting a great deal (a special price for loyal customers). There are so many inventors, copywriters, and art directors who have expended their brilliance creating these wants (as well as writers exposing their methods) I cannot compete. All salesmen know these things and more, so I will be brief: if you can make someone want something you have, you have leverage and can apply pressure. These are assets which will help you get what you want. Below are a few useful ways to create this fairytale which are especially suited to your sociopathic strengths.

FEED THE HOLE. Advertising genius makes you desperately want something you don't need, that you didn't even know existed:

Roger: "It's a substitution game. You have to remind them that they're missing something from their lives. Everyone's missing something, right?"
Nick: "I guess."
Roger: "Trust me. And when they're feeling sufficiently incomplete, you convince them your product is the only thing that can fill the void. So instead of taking steps to deal with their lives, instead of working to root out the real

reason for their misery, they go out and buy a stupid-looking pair of cargo pants."

—Dylan Kidd, *Roger Dodger*

ANCHORING. Be bold. Make the first offer and make it extremely high (if you are selling) or low (if you are buying). No matter how ridiculous this initial offer may seem, it will establish one value for the exchange that all other values will revolve around. Act like your offer is totally reasonable and supported by previous deals, but base it on how desperate the other person seems to make the exchange. Always be prepared to coolly walk away. Emphasize what they are getting instead of what they are giving up and remember, nothing is really worth anything. It's only worth how much someone else is willing to give away to get it.

FUD. Short for "Fear, Uncertainty, and Doubt" (or Disinformation), FUD is a fun and hoary negative sales technique perfect for your personality. If you can't sell something based on its merits, you can always cast doubt on your competitors by slinging shit on their products. A tactic used by industry giants such as IBM, Microsoft, and Clorox, the core idea is that if you can make someone suspicious of other products, they will be more likely to buy yours. It totally works. Try something like, "Finally, an LED lightbulb that doesn't make everything look terrible." The FUD motto: If you can't make yourself look good, make other people look bad.

FEEL, FELT, FOUND. This is a far more saccharine method you are bound to rail against at first because of its inherent cheesiness. But contain yourself and listen up. It comes to the rescue when a hard take-it-or-leave-it negotiation is off the table—when the other person isn't madly in love with your widget and is ready to walk away—and you know it. It's an empathy trap. You empathize with your customer and soften him up. And it works. Known in the sales universe as "an objection handling technique" it's taught to all Apple genius bar employees.[17] Often confronted by frustrated, confused, tech-loser customers, part of their genius lies in helping solve the customer's problem by convincing them to buy another, newer, shinier version of same-ish said frustrating-yet-amazing object. FEEL sets the trap. As in, "I understand it seems expensive and frustrating." FELT is the bait: "I felt the same way myself when I first started using the new amazing product." FOUND is the sound of the trap snapping shut—"But I found I saved a lot of time and money with the new problem-solving features of this newer more amazing version of the product . . . and it's totally worth the additional cost in the long run."

There are countless other sales techniques you can easily find in books and blogs and classes everywhere. But there's only one you will ever really need, taught to *Organization Man* author William Whyte during his early sales training in the rugged countryside of rural depression-era America. His memory of his mentor: "'Fella,' he told me, 'you will never sell anybody anything until you learn one simple thing. The man on the other side of the counter is the enemy.'"

CHAPTER 12

ENEMIES

It is in some ways more troublesome to track and swat an evasive wasp than to shoot, at close range, a wild elephant. But the elephant is more troublesome if you miss.

—C. S. Lewis, *The Screwtape Letters*

You're making good progress. Along the way, you've fucked over some colleagues, but most of the people sore at you don't count as real enemies. Neither do those who are trying to take what you have or want. That's just competition. These are the normal jostlings of life, and while they may get a little rough, be careful who you identify as an enemy. (With the above notable exception of the person across from you in a "sell" situation.) They're not going the throw a poisoned ninja star at you in the fog of night. So get over yourself. Resist concocting an overly dramatic scenario for the flair of it, as in "He's out to get me." Probably, he's not. Elevating someone to enemy status who doesn't truly deserve it is totally pointless and exhausting. When in doubt, just keep moving. If you make them an enemy, you'll have to defend against an enemy, instead of just secretly being annoyed at the little shitbag who snagged your coveted parking spot. Enemies are tiring, and will seriously tax your self-control. A proper enemy is something else. They want to skewer you through the eye with a fondue fork and are bent on discrediting and exposing you. They require special measures.

We have reached the point in the story where it's tempting to pull out the *The Art of War* and get all metaphysical for a hot second. This book offers advice which sounds quite natural to you, the sociopath:

"Appear weak when you are strong, and strong when you are weak."

"Let your plans be dark and impenetrable as night, and when you move, fall like a thunderbolt."

"In the midst of chaos, there is also opportunity"[1]

Etcetera. Just be aware, quoting this book out loud makes you sound like a loser who thinks they're Batman. When the fun is over, it's important to recognize the reality that having an "enemy" is both more complicated and more mundane.

There are two distinct ways to deal with enemies: before you make them, and once you have them. In this way, treating enemies is like dealing with STDs. Like the saying goes, "An ounce of prevention is worth a pound of cure," so the first method is best: don't make enemies. If someone is cutting you down in a way that actively challenges your position, take a deep breath and try to deal with it in a realistic and calm way; it's a lot less dramatic than what you might have expected. Enemies are for war. This is about keeping your head cool and avoid falling into the Hollywood "mortal enemy" narrative trap, which is great for cinema but terrible for your sleep cycle. In short, two rules of thumb for enemies:

1) Avoid making enemies when possible.
2) Don't prematurely conceive of someone as an enemy just because they irritate you or you hate them.

If you do find yourself with a proper enemy, stall getting into a fight for as long as you can. Use him to strengthen yourself. There's an old Buddhist saying, "An enemy is as useful as a buddha" and it's true. In *The Act of Will*, Robert Assagioli suggests using this teaching as a bulwark against time wasters, as "they teach us the art of courteous but firm refusal to engage in unnecessary conversation. To be able to say 'no' is a difficult but useful discipline." Philosopher Emil Cioran puts the use of an enemy-as-Buddha more bluntly in *The Trouble with Being Born*: "Our enemy watches over us, keeps us from letting ourselves go. By indicating, by divulging our least weaknesses, he leads us straight to our salvation, moves heaven and earth to keep us from being unworthy of his image of us. Hence our gratitude to him should be boundless." If you can frame your enemy interactions in this light (maybe without the divine salvation bit) you can use an enemy as a sparring partner, as in good old overly-quoted-yet-totally-useful-and-true Nietzsche: "That which does not kill us, makes us stronger."

KEEP YOUR FRIENDS CLOSE AND YOUR ENEMIES CLOSER

Everyone quotes this but what does it really mean? Take your frenemies to happy hour and play skeeball with the the shittiest people in your orbit? Why? Unless you're a serious mafiosi planning to marry off your daughter to some don so you can track him down and kill him and his entire family later, this aphorism isn't for you. This is the kind of horseshit people spout while pretending to be Hollywood power agents but the truth is it makes no sense. Your so-called enemies inside the office despise you, talk shit behind your back, and are looking to unseat you from afar. They don't want to come over for dinner, and even if they did, what would you do? Put ricin in their wine? They're just nasty jerks who want to get their grubby paws on what you have, so our best course of action is to treat them like any other climber jostling for your space. Do not give anyone special enemy status. Unless they really deserve it.

Enemies outside the office are constantly trying to learn what you and your company are doing. In this case, it can be entertaining to go head-to-head for a power lunch and try to pry information out of each other, but the idea of them being a friend and keeping them close—especially for someone like you—is a risky and terrible idea. Besides, Sun Tzu never said it. Michael Corleone did, and he came from Hollywood, a place flush with romantic-sounding, practically senseless lines that have no real bearing on your day at the salt mine. What Sun did say was way more sensible: "If you know the enemy and if you know yourself, your victory will not stand in doubt." These two big "ifs" are the part of all this worth remembering.

DO NOT ENGAGE. Just because he calls you his enemy, doesn't mean you must return the favor. By publicly refusing to elevate him to enemy status, you will fill him with impotent rage. He may well self-destruct and you will remain comfortably on the "right side of history."

If you must engage, there are many previously discussed ways to confound and incite outrage. Here are a few we haven't already covered:

ACTIVE MEASURES

This is a Russian KGB term used to describe secret maneuvers that go well beyond surveillance and into active subversion. For example: hacking and releasing DNC emails, breaching the Florida voting booths, contacting Trump's campaign, etc. It is "the use of leaks and disinformation to undermine the integrity, the confidence of your adversary."[2] It's a purely negative campaign intended to simply tear down your enemy. Think of it as a political version of FUD. In this past election cycle, Putin wanted to show that the West is just "as hypocritical, as cynical as Russia"[3]—that the system is as rigged here as it is there. The dirtier and messier our election was, the better. That's the key to active measures: keep focused, simple. Do not link it to lifting yourself up, simply tear the other guy down. And let public opinion do the work for you.

Active measures are not new. Since World War II, the KGB has targeted public figures such as Herbert Hoover and Martin Luther King Jr. and donated more than $1 billion of secret funds to foment the anti-Vietnam protests in the United States. All while making everybody think it was their own idea. Science has backed up philosopher Blaise Pascal's claim that "people are generally better persuaded by the reasons which they have themselves discovered than by those which have come into the mind of others."[4] Fomenting doubt is fun, fomenting incorrect certainty is even more so.

KOMPROMAT

Another, more aggressive form of the teardown also comes to us courtesy of the KGB. It takes a little more planning, involving the fabrication and planting of compromising material intended to discredit your opponent. The clandestine nature of *kompromat* is what makes it effective and powerful. According to the *New York Times*, "Old-style kompromat featured doctored photographs, planted drugs, grainy videos of liaisons with prostitutes hired by the K.G.B., and a wide range of other primitive entrapment techniques." But it's not just the KGB. The same article cites that Russian hackers "post offers on clandestine websites to plant child pornography in order to ruin reputations or get someone arrested. The going price for such a job is reportedly $600, paid in Bitcoins."[5] Learn from the best, get your untraceable currency handy, and set up a cyber teardown.

GASLIGHTING

This is a classic form of psychological manipulation as described in Patrick Hamilton's 1938 play *Gas Light* (and the film adaptation *Gaslight*) and is most effective in close relationships which suffer little outside influence, light, or air. Its effectiveness is dependent on making the other person think they're crazy, while feigning concern for their well-being and sanity. While not exactly a break-room staple, it is another indication of how effective sowing doubt can be in destabilizing someone else. It's also very difficult for someone to prove you are doing it, and is a fun word to throw around. As in:

> "Why are you gaslighting me?"
> "What?"
> "I totally sent you the files"
> "I didn't get them."
> "Why are you fucking with me? That's weird."
> "I'm not fucking with you!"
> "You're being really weird."

Where does this weird yet well-known term come from? In the play, the wife who is being gaslighted hangs on to the one piece of empirical evidence she has to prove that her husband is baiting her—the gas light:

> I can tell everything by the light of the gas. You see the mantle there. Now it's burning full. But if an extra light went on in the kitchen or someone lit it in the bedroom then this one would sink down. It's the same all over the house. . . . Every night, after he goes out, I find myself waiting for something. Then all at once I look round the room and see that the light is slowly going down. Then I hear tapping sounds. . . . I would go all over the house to see if anyone had put on an extra light, but they never had. It's always at the same time—about ten minutes after he goes out. That's what gave me the idea that somehow he had come back and that it was he who was walking about up there.[6]

Not everyone has a concrete anchoring device like the literal "gas light" to help expose what you are doing to them. Tell people your enemy is crazy.

Tell him he's crazy. Challenge his idea of sanity at every turn. As in, "You're confused Danny. You're totally batshit crazy. And Dufresne knows you're basically useless. Everyone is lying to your face. You're a drunk. You're not stable or normal." Question everything.

If you can make them worry that everyone else is thinking the same thing, so much the better. Harnessing the POWER OF PARANOIA will increase your advantage immensely.

These are rough-and-ready maneuvers that should handle most nonlethal enemies and other unrulies, hell-bent on giving you a hard time. There is, of course, one notable exception: someone just like you.

CHAPTER 13

YOU VERSUS YOU

At every party with a hundred people, there's probably a psychopath there and he's looking for weakness.

—James Fallon, *The Psychopath Inside*

Okay. Here's a worthy enemy. Spotting another sociopath is not unlike experiencing love at first sight. Except less pleasant. There is all the recognition and heightened awareness, but it's more like strolling across the veldt and spotting the lion. And he's staring at you. You begin to wonder . . . . Can two psychopaths be allies? Do you let on to one another who you really are? Can you cooperate, ever? The answer is, yes, sometimes. But in all likelihood, you aren't going to get along well at all.

There are three things you can do when you meet another sociopath. The first is to quit right away. The second is to avoid him aggressively. The third is to partner up—just be very careful. Tech start-ups and outlaw motorcycle gangs are places where multiple sociopaths can stitch together for a while, but remember, when it goes south, you could be looking at a very malevolent face-off.

You're the one who thought psychopaths were so interesting. They get tiresome after a while don't you think?

—Martin McDonagh, *Seven Psychopaths*

Carl Jung said, "The meeting of two personalities is like the contact of two chemical substances: if there is any reaction, both are transformed." During an original *Knight Rider* episode when Kitt is opposing his nemesis Karr, another supposedly indestructible automobile, Kitt asks "What happens when an indestructible object hits an immoveable object?" During a game of chicken, Karr swerves off a bridge, hits a giant rock and explodes. Question answered. Going head-to-head with another sociopath is kind of like this. It seems impossible, but one of you is going to give somehow. So focus on shoring up your position. Before you jump to the "both of us can't live" conclusion, investigate your alternatives.

HIDE YOUR HAND. Like you, your opponent has neither unlimited self-control nor infinite energy to expend on his psychopathic manipulations. Your best chance when the attack comes is to understand his methods without drawing attention to yourself. Make yourself as small as you can. Psychologist Robert Hare, working with fellow researcher Paul Babiak, showed that the "ability to recognize psychopathic manipulation is increased if you are not seen as valuable or a threat to the psychopath"[1] because he's not expending energy in order to fool you.

The key to effective sparring with another sociopath is knowing when to start. Before you call it, you have the benefit of his relative inattention in which to prepare. Once you bring up the challenge, it's on. And you're going to be in constant danger.

SHOW TENACITY. Once your fellow sociopath is on to you, you must remain vigilant, no matter what. Ken Kesey expresses this very well in *One Flew Over the Cuckoo's Nest*, a great depiction of a sociopath-on-sociopath battle: "I thought for a minute there I saw her whipped. Maybe I did. But I see now that it don't make any difference. . . . To beat her you don't have to whip her two out of three or three out of five, but every time you meet. As soon as you let down your guard, as soon as you lose *once*, she's won for good. And eventually we all got to lose. Nobody can help that." The late, great Mitch Hedberg also put it well: "The thing about tennis is: no matter how much I play, I'll never be as good as a wall. I played a wall once. They're fucking relentless." So once it's on, dig in.

DANCE WITH THE DEVIL. If staying away isn't feasible, sometimes there are ways you can work it out. Per Robert Hare: "Occasionally, however, psychopaths become temporary partners in crime . . . Generally, one member of the pair is a 'talker' who gets his or her way through charm, deceit, and manipulation, whereas the other is a 'doer' who prefers direct action—intimidation and force. As long as their interests are complementary, they make a formidable pair."[2] If you do decide to team up, look for someone with complementary personality traits and avoid getting into direct competition over the details. Stay focused on the broader objective. And try not to pick a fight.

Well, that was a short bit of bedtime reading. That's because this whole enterprise is ill-advised. Sociopath-on-sociopath is almost always a bad scene. It might be fun to cat-and-mouse with one another for a while, and it can be invigorating to spar with a worthy enemy, but understand that the conflict will only move in one direction: escalation. All humans are better at escalating than de-escalating. But you are exceptionally so. This will not end well. If you're bored picking off weak losers, and find yourself tempted to seek out a proper duel, remember to be careful what you wish for.

CHAPTER 14

WINNING

Man is the most vicious of all animals, and life is a series of battles ending in victory or defeat.

—Donald J. Trump, 1981 *People* magazine interview

What does "winning" mean in the world today? This you will have to decide for yourself. Think about the fable of Country Mouse and City Mouse. Country Mouse lives safely in a leaky barn eating stale millet. He visits City Mouse who lives in a palace and eats foie gras, only the palace is also inhabited by a ferocious cat, so the mice must always remain vigilant against sneak attacks. After a terrifying encounter with the cat, Country Mouse was like, "Forget this noise, my barn is safe and good enough for me." And City Mouse was like, "Cool, see you later. Enjoy the millet, you chickenshit." Before setting your sights on how far you want to climb within the organization, you should ask yourself how much pressure you are willing to take. Are you a City Mouse or a Country Mouse? Try to be honest with yourself. And make sure you're not acting as one while expecting the results of the other. If you are thinking, "Why the fuck are we talking about mice? I'm gonna be the cat," you are either deluded or a MASTER, destined to become a drug lord, the founder of a new religion, or a successful dictator.

THE BELTWAY

The Beltway is a country-mouse method and provides a good approach to business, if you want to protect your personal time. As a sociopath, you'll probably

146

find this route boring, but it's an option worth considering for a moment at least. Beltways were built around sprawling congested cities like Washington, DC, and Atlanta to allow you to drive from one side of the city to the other without actually going through the dense center. The Beltway approach is to skirt around the rush-hour crush of people trying to "get up." Don't set your sights on the thing everybody wants because even if you can get it, everyone will be trying to steal it from you. Instead of the corner office, what about the one next door? You will have a lot more peace, and it still has a window. Ultimately, if you can find a way to enjoy the things nobody else really wants, you can make yourself very comfortable without getting caught up in the rat race. If you need excitement, find it somewhere else. If you aim to thrive, but don't look to domination as the core of your satisfaction, find the Beltway.

THE TOP OF THE PYRAMID

You find your satisfaction in crushing and winning. City Mouse, this is you, angling for the top, the peak, head honcho, VIP, big league, CEO. This is

about going for and getting the brass ring. And then keeping it. Take what you've learned in this book about pressure, presentation of self, confidence, competence, spillover, etc., and plot your course. There's one thing you should prepare yourself for as you climb the ladder, which Jerry Useem shows in *Why It Pays to Be a Jerk* the higher you climb, "the more frequent the acts of aggression . . . until, near the very top, aggression ceases almost completely."[1] There's nobody left. It's quiet up here.

From this vantage, you can become a master who quietly controls everything so that everyone does what you tell them to, and they *want* to do it. This is the rarefied air at the very top of the pyramid. The ultimate kind of winning.

To build on the skills already discussed throughout this book, think about how you can improve your visionary persuasive powers. Having great vision is a gift. But you can improve your visionary IQ by practicing a few things which will aid you in becoming a master.

> I'm not bi-polar. I'm bi-winning. I win here and I win there . . . I'm tired of pretending I'm not special. I'm tired of pretending I'm not a total bitchin' rock star from Mars.
>
> —Charlie Sheen

THINK BIGGER

This is hard for many people to do. As they get set in their ways, they also get set in their idea of what is possible. But because the future is wildly undetermined, this belief is absurd. Remember, when faced with something you want to do but "isn't done" ask yourself "why not?" Is it impossible? Is it illegal? Or is it just not customary? It will rarely be the first. The second might be dangerous for you. But if it's just not customary, try it out. You'll get away with more than you think. Here's an example from Louis CK:

> I rented a car a couple weeks ago . . . and then when I went home, I had to drop the car at the rental place—you know you gotta go to the rental place that's off the airport, give them the car, give them your thing with the mileage, you got to get on a bus and then go to your terminal and check in—I was late and I was worried about missing my

flight so I knew I had no time to do any of that so I just—I never did this before—I just drove my car right to the terminal and just left it there. And I got on the plane. And once I was on the plane and I had a little moment I called Hertz and I said, "Hey listen your car is sitting out in front of terminal four and the keys are in it. So, that's where it is." And the guy was like, "You can't do that. You have to return it to this location and then get . . . " And I go "Well, I didn't do that already. And now I'm leaving California. So if you want your car you need to go to that place where it is." And he was like "Aw Jesus, man. All right. We'll get it." And he—that was the end of it—and I realized I could do this every time.

SCULPT MEMORY

We, amnesiacs all, condemned to live in an eternally fleeting present, have created the most elaborate of human constructions, memory, to buffer ourselves against the intolerable knowledge of the irreversible passage of time and the irretrievability of its moments and events . . . There is only experience and its decay.

—Geoffrey Sonnabend[2]

The instability and malleability of memory enables you to monkey around with someone's mind.

Memory is surprisingly fluid and frail. There are many ways you can exploit memory biases to encourage someone to misremember in your favor. You can even make them have new memories. Amnesia is when you forget everything, but paramnesias or false memories also happen. Encourage others to remember something that never happened, and you can make them believe anything. We are a highly suggestible species. Remember cognitive fluency? Well, you can use it here: suggest a false memory you want them to have. The more familiar and plausible sounding you can make the false memory, the more believable it will seem:

"Dave told us he had all the files, remember?"

"Hmmm . . . I don't."

"We were by the copy machine. It jammed. And Rose got all flustered?"

"Ha, Rose and that machine are something else."

"I know, right? Anyway, Dan came by and tried to help, with his jelly doughnut dripping onto his shirt . . ."

"Oh yeah . . . sounds familiar."

"Remember?"

"I think so, yeah . . . OK yeah, I do remember. Damn."

Some scientists even suggest that extreme cognitive fluency is the cause of déjà vu: you are experiencing something so familiar you believe you are remembering it as it's occurring.[3] If you could induce a déjà vu, now that would be some freaky shit.

MISATTRIBUTIONS. These are memory lapses where you remember something, but forget how you experienced it.[4] The phenomenon is sometimes called SOURCE CONFUSION. Did you see it on TV? Were you there? If you can make someone remember being somewhere, when in reality they only heard about it later, you can make them feel more responsible for a decision or mistake. As in "Why didn't you say so when we were all there deciding to do it?"

CRYPTOMNESIA. You read something, saw something, heard a really cool story, but forgot about it. Later you remember the cool story, but not where it came from, so you think it's your own imaginative idea and retell it as such. It's a common phenomenon, so feel free to use it as an excuse. Grab a great idea from someone else and run with it. If you happen to be accused of copying her story, simply say, "The premises may seem awfully similar, I agree, but I don't remember encountering the story before. If I read her account and repeated it, it must be a case of cryptomnesia." The accuser won't understand what you just said, so they'll believe practically anything you want them to.

PERSISTENCE. This memory bias causes awful events to be remembered repeatedly. If you can stage an awful event, you can really ravage someone's mental state with it, basically inducing PTSD.

PEAK-END RULE.[5] Another memory bias you can exploit by making sure to go out with a bang. People remember how things wrap up, and tend to rate the overall experience based on how it ends. Finish strong and use the early stages of a projet to dick around and get what you need done for yourself.

ROSY RETROSPECTION. This bias can help you smooth things over. Just reach back deep into the past to a familiar time or event, drop a "remember when," and let it go to work. We are hardwired to remember the past as being better than it was, so with a gentle reminder, you can get any asshole to start spouting off like a senile old man. "In my day, we didn't have all this Internet garbage. Life was simpler then. Things were simpler. America was great." Every generation does this. You will leave him reminiscing in a fog of nostalgia over a lost time and he will forget why he was screeching at you just a moment ago.

SPREAD MIND VIRUSES

When you hear the word MEME, you'll probably think of the disgruntled cat photos and manic dance videos which explode across the Internet daily. Or a six-word tweet that is retweeted tens of millions of times by breakfast. But there's a deeper reason we casually call the phenomenon "going viral." Evolutionary biologist Richard Dawkins coined the word to describe a stable idea or unit of thought that spreads from one mind to the other without being altered or destroyed. Basically, the meme uses the human mind to replicate itself and spread by "cultural transmission" much the same way a virus uses a cell. It sounds kind of crazy, but memes are stunningly effective. Once properly introduced you can't unthink them. As genetic mutation is to evolution, memes are to cultural evolution. For example, Dawkins describes religion as a memetic virus.[6] It has spread for thousands of years even though he says, "Faith is the great cop-out, the great excuse to evade the need to think and evaluate evidence. Faith is belief in spite of, even perhaps because of, the lack of evidence." Wait. This sounds familiar. Remember the backfire effect? Cognitive bias?

Memes are like bias on steroids, let loose in collective thought. Ideas with power. People who invent and accelerate the spread of memes are sometimes called "cultural entrepreneurs" or "folk devils."[7] A craze (think Beatlemania), a cultural revolution (hippies or chairman Mao), and the new must-have piece of technology (the first iPhone, advertising) are all memes. More significantly for you, because of its easy handle-ability and rapid transmission, you can weaponize a meme. Like mental ebola, a properly launched, malevolent set of memes can cause mayhem like moral panics (the war on drugs), mass hysteria (the Salem witch trials), or even world war (Nazis).

As you can glean from above, many great memetic entrepreneurs are brother sociopaths. The best of them launch subterranean attacks on the collective mind. But even if you have no interest in being a meme creator or promoter in the culture, you can still use this concept to subtly manipulate those around you.

In the book, Virus of the Mind, Richard Brodie explains, "If you better understand how your mind works, you can better navigate through a world of increasingly subtle manipulation." The reverse is also true—the better you understand how others' minds work, the more subtly you can manipulate them. Tend the cosmic dark garden. Offer society its night terrors.

Gossip is a great way to use memetics to ruin someone's reputation. It's simple, moves incredibly quickly, defies the usual channels of organizational hierarchy, and isn't subject to rigorous fact checking. You can make something up out of the blue and simply say, "I heard Jeff spotted Dan and Fran sucking face at the Alibi Lounge last night." By the time word gets back, even if Jeff denies it rigorously, it will be too late for the other two. Dan and Fran will be forever linked, in the minds of others, to a night that never was.

The most powerful belief, as we've discussed before, is one a person thinks he's found for himself. Christopher Nolan expressed the difficulty of planting this kind of belief in his film *Inception,* where only a master can foster a belief in your mind without you realizing it. Inception, in this sense, is the ability, not only to make someone think they want to do what you want them to do, but that it's actually their own original idea, based on a deeply held belief about who they really are. Nolan expanded the meaning of the word inception from the simpler idea that it means origin point or beginning:

> **Saito:** "Inception. Is it possible? If you can steal an idea from someone's mind, why can't you plant one there instead?"
> **Arthur:** "Okay, here's planting an idea: I say to you, 'Don't think about elephants,' what are you thinking about?"
> **Saito:** "Elephants."
> **Arthur:** "Right. But it's not your idea because you know I gave it to you."
> **Saito:** "You could plant it subconsciously."
> **Arthur:** "The subject's mind can always trace the genesis of the idea. True inspiration is impossible to fake."
> **Cobb:** "No, it isn't. You need the simplest version of the idea, the one that will grow naturally in the subject's mind. Subtle art."

Despots want to have this level of control over people, but they usually need to resort to violence, brainwashing, and fear. Occasionally, they succeed, as George Orwell described in *1984*: "But it was all right, everything was all right, the struggle was finished. He had won the victory over himself. He loved Big Brother." The TRUE MASTER doesn't need to use this kind of coercion. Many times you don't even know who he is. And if you do know him, you love him, all on your own.

LESSONS FROM A MASTER: PABLO ESCOBAR

Pablo Escobar was a true master. At one time "El Patron de Mal" was the seventh richest man in the world. He enjoyed massive popular loyalty and years after his death is still beloved by thousands. Many consider "Pablito" the greatest outlaw of the twentieth century. For a narco-terrorist who ordered the killing of thousands (including six hundred police officers and a presidential candidate), had enemies burned and cut to pieces, and blew up a commercial 727 jet with 107 innocent passengers on board, he sure has a lot of fans.

How did he do it?

MAGNANIMITY

> Only power can get people into a position where they may be noble.
>
> —Alfred Kazin

Escobar had remarkable charisma and, when he felt like it, showed excellent character and genuine regard for others. You'll recognize some of his behaviors as those discussed in this book. "When I first met Escobar it was like I had seen a god. He had this huge presence, like an aura around him," says Popeye, Escobar's number-one assassin who planned three thousand murders, executing three hundred by his own hand. "He just knew how people worked. Don Pablo was a very respectful man to those who gave it to him. He would *capture people's minds* through the affection he could show them as a friend. . . . He never shouted once, never made snide remarks, nothing, he was a clear man. He spoke slowly, with a lot of respect, he looked everyone in the eye when he spoke to them."[8]

Popeye says this about a man who asked him to murder his own girlfriend: "If Pablo Escobar were born again, I would join him without a moment's hesitation. . . . He was loved by us. He taught us to fight and gave us everything."[9] Popeye's love for Escobar is that of a man who could kill and never lose a night's sleep. For Popeye, killing "was simply like a day at the office." A relationship between two sociopaths is difficult to pull off but can be immensely rewarding.

GENEROSITY

Pablo provided massive spillover, not just for his crew, but for a much wider swath of the population, including the powerless and desperately poor. There's a neighborhood in his home city named in his honor, and people still sell shirts and trinkets emblazoned with his face. "It's like wearing a [picture] of a saint you have faith in," says one local. He helped thousands, and not surprisingly, their tangible gain was more important to them than the fates of strangers. "We respect the pain of his victims, but we ask people to understand our joy and gratitude, what it means to move out from a garbage dump to a decent house," says another resident of Barrio Pablo Escobar.[10] Pablito had so much to spill over that he ended up burying stacks of cash and treasure in secret caves all over the countryside.

SMARTS

Pablo said he sometimes felt like a god because he could order a killing and it would go down the same day. Even so, he didn't let success go to his head. He always remained clever and careful. At some point, he was on the run and practically cornered. Hunted by the government and enemy cartels, and wanted in the United States, he agreed to surrender and serve a five-year sentence, with three conditions: 1) he could design his own prison; 2) he could pick his own guards; and 3) he wouldn't be extradited to the United States. Thrilled to have caught him, the government agreed and built him "la Catedral," a prison carefully designed to keep assassins out and the drug trade up and running. Set on a hill above his hometown and boasting a soccer field, Jacuzzis, and a chapel, Pablo could see his daughter at her window while they talked together on the phone. It's not surprising the locals called la Catedral "Hotel Escobar."

Most of the time, he knew when to restrain himself. But then he arranged for four enemies to be brought in and murdered within the prison walls. Even a master sometimes makes mistakes. This one Pablito paid for with his life.

The Columbian Army surrounded la Catedral, intending to take Escobar back into custody. But Pablo vanished. Some say he simply walked out the back gate, others that he broke through a specially designed portion of the perimeter wall. Either way, he was gone. For sixteen months the police, army, vigilante groups, and rival cartel members all searched for him in vain.

"The phone is death," Pablo had often said, and tracking his phone is in fact how his enemies eventually caught up with him. He was talking to his son when he heard his pursuers at the safe house door. Escobar escaped to the roof, but that is where he met his end. He had once vowed to shoot himself in the right ear before being taken alive, and his son said "my father told me he had fifteen bullets in his pistol; fourteen were for his enemies and the last one for him."[11] And so Pablo was found on the rooftop: the fatal shot to his right ear, his pistol by his side. Even death only improved his image. He remains a master from beyond the grave.

Joaquín "El Chapo" Guzmán was also for a time the most powerful drug trafficker in the world. He protected thousands, killed thousands, escaped spectacularly from prison multiple times with the help of his tunneling henchmen, and had a stronghold in the Sinaloa mountains. But in some ways, El Chapo was

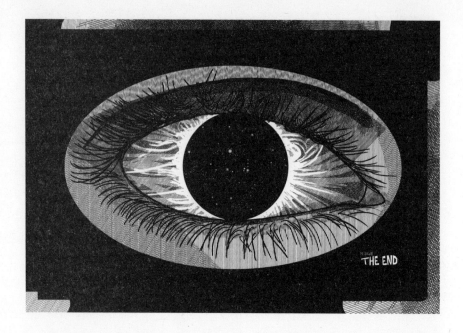

a wannabe who Escobar got tripped up by his own hubris. He wanted producers to make movies about him. A true master makes the producers do the wanting.

Guzmán was starfucked enough to invite Sean Penn to interview him for *Rolling Stone*, risking his own security and that of his men. He was caught because "he established communication with actors and producers, which formed a new line of investigation."[12] He is currently in jail in New York where tunneling is difficult. Note: mastery is extremely hard to achieve. Trying to force it will only get you in trouble. Let this be a lesson to you.

You don't need to run a cartel to be a master. It's not about scale, it's about getting people to do what you want them to do because they want to. This is mastery. A subtle art. Mastery is separated from coercion and all other openly forceful and threatening techniques. It's not just winning because you have a bigger weapon. It's winning, with everyone rooting for you.

We would rather talk to the people who manipulate the puppets.

—Robert Mugabe

EPILOGUE

I gave you everything you could ask for and you fucked it all up.

—O. J. Simpson

Hunter S. Thompson eventually got the shit beat out of him by the Hell's Angels. So let us end where we began. You are part of the one percenters, the sociopaths. Across the board, human beings have an astonishing capacity to be dicks, but you're the real deal. Special. Uparalleled. So take care of yourself, and remember: "Individuals with antisocial personality disorder are more likely than people in the general population to die prematurely by violent means."[1] So look both ways before crossing the alley.

By reading this book, I hope you've learned ways to hone your attention and manipulate beliefs. To exploit cognitive biases, actively engage in measures to destabilize those around you, and generally confound and amaze. You are the antidote to cute. If you can get everyone off-balance and scrambling, while you stay cool and in charge, you can get anything you want.

There is so much more to say, but I have to cap it off. Follow the threads I have laid. You now have a vocabulary and shorthand to help further your studies into frail and biased human cognitive mechanisms, and how to exploit them. My hope is that you will no longer be stressed about manipulating people, and will have the tools required to stay hidden and to prosper. Rest assured, the time is ripe. Truth and reason are in the trash pile. Rhetoric is heated. Reading is down, history unremembered, narcissism and bias enabled. People are caged in reflexive crouches of neuroticism, relativism, and fear. With the attention span of gnats. Sociopaths, this is the time to strike. Go forth and get what you want because you want it. Don't be shy.

THANKS

Many thanks to Joseph Craig, Andrew Stuart, and Captain Tusk, who believed in this project and helped get it off the ground. Special thanks to Doctor K., Laura Avery, Anne Carkeet, Alec Hammond, Angela Gygi, Jared Kurt, Orange Julius, M. H., Stephanie Little, and Moses Chambers, who provided great insight and support. Finally, thanks to all the anonymous sources and quoted scholars who contributed to this book, whether they knew it, approved it, or not; especially Erving Goffman, who is a genius.

SELECTED BIBLIOGRAPHY

American Psychiatry Association. *Diagnostic and Statistical Manual of Mental Disorders, Fifth Edition.* Arlington VA: American Psychiatric Association, 2013.

Babiak, P. and R. Hare. *Snakes in Suits: When Psychopaths Go to Work.* New York: Harper-Collins e-books, 2006.

Carnegie, Dale. *How to Win Friends and Influence People.* New York: Simon and Schuster, 1936. Reprint hardcover edition, 2009.

Chase, Stuart. *Guides to Straight Thinking; With 13 Common Fallacies.* New York: Harper, 1956.

Cleckley, Hervey, M.D., *The Mask of Sanity, An Attempt to Clarify Some Issues About the So-Called Psychopathic Personality.* Augusta, Georgia: Medical College of Georgia, 3rd-Edition, 1955.

Cohen, Stanley. *Folk Devils and Moral Panics.* New York: MacGibbon and Kee Ltd, 1972. Republished by Routledge, 2011.

Cuddy, Amy. *Presence: Bringing Your Boldest Self to Your Biggest Challenges.* New York: Little, Brown and Company, 2015.

Dutton, Kevin. *The Wisdom of Psychopaths. What Saints, Spies and Serial Killers Can Teach Us about Success.* New York: Farrar, Straus and Giroux, 2012.

Fallon, James. *The Psychopath Inside: A Neuroscientist's Personal Journey into the Dark Side of the Brain.* New York: Penguin Publishing Group, 2013.

Frankfurt, Harry G. *On Bullshit.* Princeton, New Jersey: Princeton University Press, 2005.

Gladwell, Malcolm. *Blink: The Power of Thinking Without Thinking.* New York: Little, Brown and Company, 2005.

Goffman, Erving. *The Presentation of Self in Everyday Life.* New York: Anchor Books, 1959.

Grant, Adam. *Give and Take: Why Helping Others Drives Our Success.* New York: Viking, 2013.

Greene, Robert. *The Art of Seduction.* New York: Penguin, 2001.

Halvorson, Heidi Grant. *No One Understands You and What to Do About It.* Boston, Massachusetts: Harvard Business Review Press, 2015.

Hamilton, Patrick. "Gas Light." 1939. Published in the USA as "Angel Street: A Victorian Thriller in Three Acts." New York: A Samuel French Acting Edition, 1942.

Hare, Robert D. *Without Conscience*. New York: Pocket Books, 1995.

Heller, Joseph. *Catch 22*. New York: Simon & Schuster, 1955.

Houston, Philip and Michael Floyd, Susan Carnicero. *Spy the Lie*. New York: St. Martin's Press, 2012.

James, Oliver. *Office Politics: How to Thrive in a World of Lying, Backstabbing and Dirty Tricks*. London, UK: Vermilion, 2013.

Johnson, Ron. *The Psychopath Test*. New York: Penguin Publishing Group, 2011.

Korda, Michael. *Power! How to Get It. How to Use It*. New York: Random House, 1975.

Lyons, Dan. *Disrupted: My Misadventure in the Start-Up Bubble*. New York: Hachette Books, 2016.

McNab, Andy, and Kevin Dutton. *The Good Psychopath's Guide to Success*. London, UK: Transworld Publishers. 2014.

Orwell, George. *Down and Out in Paris and London*. New York: Houghton Mifflin Harcourt. 1972.

Orwell, George. "Politics and the English Language." London, UK: *Horizon*, 1946.

Pennebaker, James W. *The Secret Life of Pronouns: What Our Words Say About Us*. New York: Bloomsbury Press, 2011.

Schacter, Daniel L. *Seven Sins of Memory: How the Mind Forgets and Remembers*. New York: Houghton Mifflin, 2001.

Stout, Martha, PhD. *The Sociopath Next Door*. New York: Broadway Books, 2005.

Sutton, Robert I. *The No Asshole Rule: Building a Civilized Workplace and Surviving One That Isn't*. New York: Hachette Publishing Group, 2007.

Thaler, Richard H. and Cass R. Sunstein, *Nudge*. New York: Penguin, 2009.

Tzu, Sun. *The Art of War*.

Useem, Jerry. "Why It Pays to Be a Jerk." *The Atlantic*. http://www.theatlantic.com/magazine/archive/2015/06/why-it-pays-to-be-a-jerk/392066/.

Whyte, William H. *The Organization Man*. New York: Simon and Schuster, 1956. Reprint University of Pennsylvania Press, 2002.

ENDNOTES

INTRODUCTION

1 Adam Grant, *Give and Take: Why Helping Others Drives Our Success* (Viking, 2013), 17.

2 Tomas Chamorro-Premuzic, "The Dark Side of Charisma," *Harvard Business Review*, https://hbr.org/2012/11/the-dark-side-of-charisma (accessed November 2016).

3 Dale Carnegie, *How to Win Friends and Influence People* (Simon and Schuster, 1936). Reprint hardcover edition, 2009), 76.

CHAPTER 1

1 Theodore Millon, et al., *Psychopathy: Antisocial, Criminal and Violent Behavior*, 1998. "Historical Conceptions of Psychopathy in the United States and Europe," 3.

2 C.R.P. Boddy, "Corporate psychopaths and organizational type," *Journal of Public Affairs* 10 (2010): 300-310. J.M. Twenge, et al., "Birth cohort increases in psychopathology among young Americans, 1938–2007: A cross- temporal meta-analysis of the MMPI," *Clinical Psychology Review* 30 (2010): 145-54.

3 Megan Drillinger, "Signs Someone You Know Is a Psychopath in Disguise," Huffington Post, http://www.huffingtonpost.com/thrillist/signs-someone-you-know-is_b_9168796.html (accessed April 2016).
Macrina Cooper-White, "11 Signs You May Be Dating A Sociopath," Huffington Post: http://www.huffingtonpost.com/2013/08/23/11-signs-dating-a-sociopath_n_3780417.html (accessed April 2016).
Paula Carrasquillo, "On Dating A Sociopath," Huffington Post, http://www.huffingtonpost.com/2013/06/28/paula-carrasquillo-dating-sociopath_n_3518596.html (accessed April 2016).
Wray Herbert, "Psychopath. Successful Psychopath," Huffington Post, http://www.huffingtonpost.com/wray-herbert/psychopath-successful-psy_b_6955072.html (accessed April 2016).

161

Michael Shammas, "These Are the 10 Most Psychopathic Jobs in America," Huffington Post, http://www.huffingtonpost.com/mike-shammas/these-are-the-10-most-psy_b_4740345.html (accessed April 2016).

4 Robert D. Hare, "Predators: The Disturbing World of the Psychopaths among Us," *Psychology Today* 27 (1994): 54–61; Martha Stout, *The Sociopath Next Door,* quoted on cover. (Broadway Books, 2005); American Psychiatric Association: *Diagnostic and Statistical Manual of Mental Disorders*, Fifth Edition. Arlington, VA, American Psychiatric Association, 2013, 693.

5 James Fallon, *The Psychopath Inside* (New York: Penguin, 2013), 15.

6 I. Walker, "Psychopaths in Suits," Australian Broadcasting Corporation, 2005.

7 Jonathan Pearlman, "1 in 5 CEOs are Psychopaths, Study Finds," *The Telegraph*, http://www.telegraph.co.uk/news/2016/0913/1-in-5-ceos-are-psychopaths-australian-study-finds/ (accessed March 2017).

8 Kent A. Kiehl and Morris B. Hoffman, "The Criminal Psychopath: History, Neuroscience, Treatment, and Economics," *Jurimetrics* 51 (Summer 2011): 355–97.

9 Ibid.

10 James Fallon, *The Psychopath Inside,* 9.

11 Ron Johnson, "Strange Answers to the Psychopath Test" TED Ideas Worth Spreading: https://www.ted.com/talks/jon_ronson_strange_answers_to_the_psychopath_test/transcript?language=en (accessed March 2017).

12 Robert D. Hare, *Without Conscience*, 5.

13 James Strachey (trans), *The Standard Edition of the Complete Psychological Works of Sigmund Freud,* Volume XX1, "Dostoevsky and Parricide" (The Hogarth Press and the Institute of Psycho-Analysis, 1961), 178.

14 Hervey Cleckley, M.D., *The Mask Of Sanity: An Attempt To Clarify Some Issues About the So Called Psychopathic Personality,* 3rd Edition Preface, 1955, 11.

15 Cathy Spatz Widom, "A Methodology for Studying Noninstitutionalized Psychopaths," *Journal of Consulting and Clinical Psychology* 45, no. 4 (1977): 674-83.

16 Robert D. Hare, *Without Conscience,* 33–34.

17 Ron Johnson, *The Psychopath Test,* (Penguin Publishing Group, 2011), 101–102.

18 Scott A. Lillenfeld, Scott A., Ashley Watts, "Not all psychopaths are criminals - some psychopathic traits are actually linked to success," *The Conversation*, http://theconversation.com/not-all-psychopaths-are-criminals-some-psychopathic-traits-are-actually-linked-to-success-51282 (accessed March 2017).

19 Ron Johnson, *The Psychopath Test,* 123.

20 James Fallon, *The Psychopath Inside: A Neuroscientist's Personal Journey Into the Dark Side of the Brain,* (Penguin Publishing Group, 2013), 226.

21 NOTE: the *DSM-V* does have a further-evolved definition in section III as an "emerging diagnosis," which reads a lot like Hare.

22 D. Jones and D. Palhus, D., "Different Provocations Trigger Aggression in Narcissists and Psychopaths," *Social Psychological and Personality Science* (2010).

23 Scott A. Bonn, "How to Tell a Sociopath from a Psychopath," *Psychology Today*, https://www.psychologytoday.com/blog/wicked-deeds/201401/how-tell-sociopath-psychopath accessed March 2017).

24 James Fallon, *The Psychopath Inside.*

25 Kevin Dutton, *The Wisdom of Psychopaths: What Saints, Spies and Serial Killers can Teach Us about Success,* (Farrar, Straus and Giroux, 2012), (Kindle, location 1027).

26 Ernest Hemingway, as quoted in *The New Yorker*, November 30, 1929.

27 Cathy Spatz Widom, "A Methodology."

28 Robert D. Hare, *Without Conscience*, 69.

29 P. Cherulnik; J. Way; S. Ames; D. Hutto, "Impressions of high and low Machiavellian men," *Journal of Personality* 49, no. 4 (1981): 388–400.

30 Heidi Grant Halvorson, *No One Understands You and What to Do About It,* (Harvard Business Review Press, 2015). e-Book 2015, (Kindle location 723).

31 D.L. Paulhus, "Interpersonal and Intrapsychic Adaptiveness of Trait Self-Enhancement: a Mixed Blessing?" *Journal of Personality and Social Psychology* 74 (1998): pp.1197–208.

32 M. Levenson; K. Kiehl; C. Fitzpatrick, "Assessing psychopathic attributes in a noninstitutionalized population," *Journal of Personality and Social Psychology* 68 (1995): 151–158.

33 William Hirstein, "What Is a Psychopath?" *Psychology Today*, https://www.psychologytoday.com/blog/mindmelding/201301/what-is-psychopath-0 (accessed January 2017).

34 Scott A. McGreal, "Emotional Intelligence Not Relevant to Psychopaths," *Psychology Today*, https://www.psychologytoday.com/blog/unique-everybody-else/201209/emotional-intelligence-not-relevant-psychopaths (accessed March 2017).

35 Scott A. McGreal, "Are Psychopaths Really Smarter Than the Rest of Us?" *Psychology Today*, https://www.psychologytoday.com/blog/unique-everybody-else/201612/are-psychopaths-really-smarter-the-rest-us (accessed April 2017).

36 Jerry Useem, "Why It Pays to Be a Jerk," *The Atlantic*, http://www.theatlantic.com/magazine/archive/2015/06/why-it-pays-to-be-a-jerk/392066/ (accessed October 2016).

CHAPTER 2

1 Many studies, including: C. Lord; L. Ross; M. Lepper; "Biased Assimilation and Attitude Polarization: The Effects of Prior Theories on Subsequently Considered Evidence," *Journal of Personality and Social Psychology* 37, no. 11: 2098–2109.

2 Heidi Grant Halvorson. *No One Understands You:* (Kindle location 439).

3 Ibid., (Kindle location: 283).

4 Chris, "The Truth Effect and Other Processing Fluency Miracles," *Science Blogs*, http://scienceblogs.com/mixingmemory/2007/09/18/the-truth-effect-and-other-pro/ (accessed March 2016).

5 Ibid.

6   B. Fischhoff, and R. Beyth, "'I knew it would happen': Remembered probabilities of once-future things," *Organizational Behaviour and Human Performance* 13 (1975), 1-16.

CHAPTER 3

1   Jerry Useem, "Why It Pays to Be A Jerk."
2   P. Babiak, R. Hare, *Snakes in Suits: When Psychopaths Go to Work*, (Harper-Collins e-books, 2006), 10.
3   Jon Ronson, *The Psychopath Test*, 110. Quoting Robert Hare.
4   P. Babiak, R. Hare, *Snakes in Suits*, 201.
5   Eric Ries, *The Lean Startup: How Today's Entrepreneurs Use Continuous Innovation to Create Radically Successful Businesses* (Crown, 2011).
6   Dan Lyons, *Disrupted: My Misadventure in the Start-Up Bubble* (Hachette Books, 2016), 123–124.
7   http://explorepahistory.com/hmarker.php?markerId=1-A-1AB (accessed April 2017).
8   Ellen Cushing, "The Smartest Bro In the Room," *San Francisco Magazine*, http://www.modernluxury.com/san-francisco/story/the-smartest-bro-the-room#sthash.OMBeFg4j.dpuf (accessed April 2017).
9   Mike Isaac, "Inside Uber's Aggressive, Unrestrained Workplace Culture," *The New York Times*, https://www.nytimes.com/2017/02/22/technology/uber-workplace-culture.html (accessed September 2017).
10 Mike Issac, "Uber Faces Inquiry Over Use of Greyball Tool to Evade Authorities," *The New York Times*, https://www.nytimes.com/2017/05/04/technology/uber-federal-inquiry-software-greyball.html (accessed May 2017).
11 Lucinda Shen, "Travis Kalanick Is Still Worth Billions After Resigning From Uber," *Fortune*, fortune.com/2017/06/21/travis-kalanick-net-worth-billions/ (accessed September 2017).
12 Kevin Dutton, *The Wisdom of Psychopaths*, Location: 2512.
13 James Fallon, "The Psychopath Inside," 54.
14 Robert D. Hare, *Without Conscience*, 76.
15 P. Babiak, R. Hare, *Snakes in Suits*, 241.
16 Jason Beghe, as quoted in *Going Clear: Scientology and the Prison of Belief* Alex Gibney, HBO, 2015; Beghe, Jason "Speaking Freely," https://www.youtube.com/watch?v=KHbOBZyF5OK (accessed September 2017).
17 Lauren Weber, "Today's Personality Tests Raise the Bar for Job Seekers," *Wall Street Journal*, http://www.wsj.com/articles/a-personality-test-could-stand-in-the-way-of-your-next-job-1429065001 (accessed April 2017).
18 Ibid.
19 William H. Whyte, *The Organization Man* (Simon and Schuster, 1956.) Reprint University of Pennsylvania Press, 2002, 405.
20 Ibid., 405–406.

21 Dan P. McAdams, "The Mind of Donald Trump," *The Atlantic*, http://www.theatlantic.com/magazine/archive/2016/06/the-mind-of-donald-trump/480771/ (Accessed August 2016).

22 William H. Whyte, *The Organization Man,* 122.

23 Dan P. McAdams, "The Mind of Donald Trump."

24 Gary Fields, John R.Emshwiller, "As Arrest Records Rise, Americans Find Consequences Can Last A Lifetime," *The Wall Street Journal*, http://www.wsj.com/articles/as-arrest-records-rise-americans-find-consequences-can-last-a-lifetime-1408415402 (accessed March 2017).

CHAPTER 4

1   James Uleman, As quoted by Mark Rowh. "First Impressions Count," American Psychological Association: http://www.apa.org/gradpsych/2012/11/first-impressions.aspx (accessed January 2017.)

2   Richard H. Thaler; Cass R. Sunstein, *Nudge: Improving Decisions About Health, Wealth, and Happiness* (Penguin Publishing Group, 2008), 19.

3   Amy Cuddy, *Presence: Bringing Your Boldest Self to Your Biggest Challenges* (Little, Brown and Company, 2015), 21.

4   Erving Goffman, *The Presentation of Self In Everyday Life* (Anchor Books, 1959).

5   Michael Korda, *Power! How to Get It. How to Use It* (Random House, 1975).

6   George Orwell, *1984* (Penguin Publishing Group, 1950).

7   Unattributed, "Making Murder Respectable," *The Economist*, http://www.economist.com/node/21541767 (accessed February 2017).

8   Joseph Heller, *Catch 22* (Simon & Schuster, 2011), 552.

9   Amy Cuddy, *Presence,* 147.

10 Amy Cuddy, "Your Body Language Shapes Who You Are," TED Talks: https://www.youtube.com/watch?v=Ks-_Mh1QhMc (accessed March 2016).

11 Tanya L. Chartrand and John A. John A in "The chameleon effect: The perception-behavior link and social interaction," *The Journal of Personality and Social Psychology* 76 no. 6 (Jun 1999): 893–910.

12 Nia-Malika Henerson, "Blacks, whites hear Obama differently," *Politico*, http://www.politico.com/story/2009/03/blacks-whites-hear-obama-differently-019538 (accessed March 2016).

13 Sandra Blakeslee,"Mind Games: Sometimes a White Coat Isn't Just a White Coat," *New York Times*, http://www.nytimes.com/2012/04/03/science/clothes-and-self-perception.html (accessed April 2017).

14 Ibid.

15 Michael Korda, *Power!*.

16 Sara Goldsmith, "The Rise of the Fork," *Slate*, http://www.slate.com/articles/arts/design/2012/06/the_history_of_the_fork_when_we_started_using_forks_and_how_their_design_changed_over_time_.html (accessed Februard 2017).

17 Michael Korda, *Power!*.

18 Tamara Rakic, "Psychologists show how accent shapes our perception of a person," *Science News*, https://www.sciencedaily.com/releases/2010/12/101217145649.htm (Accessed March 2017).
19 Matt Dathan, "Does Your Accent Really Hinder Your Job Prospects?" *Guardian*, https://www.theguardian.com/careers/accent-hinder-job-prospects (accessed October 2016).
20 Heidi Grant Halvorson, *No One Understands You,* (Kindle location 437).
21 Ibid., (Kindle Locations 405–406).
22 Kate DuBose Tomassi, "Most Common Resume Lies," *Forbes*: http://www.forbes.livepage.apple.comcom/2006/05/20/resume-lies-work_cx_kdt_06work_0523lies.html (accessed November 2016).
23 Ibid.

CHAPTER 5

1 R. Christie; F. Geis, *Studies in Machiavellianism*, (New York: Academic Press, 1970).
2 https://en.wikipedia.org/wiki/Regulatory_focus_theory.
3 Stephanie Loiacono, "Rules the Warren Buffet Lives By," Investopedia: http://finance.yahoo.com/news/pf_article_108903.html (accessed October 2016).
4 Steve Berglas, "10 Myths About Successful Entrepreneurs--Debunked," *Forbes*, https://www.forbes.com/sites/stevenberglas/2012/03/02/ten-myths-about-suc-cessful-entrepreneurs-debunked/3/#57228b6f1c94 (accessed Ferbruary 2017.)
5 Robert I. Sutton, *The No Asshole Rule - Building a Civilized Workplace and Surviving One That Isn't,* (Hachette Publishing Group, 2007). (Kindle Location 1781).
6 M. Crawford, A. McConnell, A. Lewis, S. Sherman, "Reactance, Compliance and Anticipated Regret," *Journal of Experimental Social Psychology* 38 (2002): 56–63.
7 Jerry Useem, Jerry, "Why It Pays to Be A Jerk."
8 Adam Grant, *Give and Take*, 7.
9 Ibid., 7.
10 F. Flynn; V. Lake, "If You Need Help, Just Ask: Underestimating Compliance with Direct Requests for Help," *Journal of Personality and Social Psychology* 95 no. 1 (2008): 128–143.
11 A.W. Brooks, F. Gino, and M.E. Schweitzer, "Smart People Ask for (My) Advice: Seeking Advice Boosts Perceptions of Competence," *Management Science* 61, no. 6 (June 2015): 1421–1435.
12 D. Katz, A. Caplan, J. Merz, "All Gifts Large and Small: Toward an Understanding of the Ethics of Pharmaceutical Industry Gift-Giving," *The American Journal of Bioethics* 3, no. 3 (2003):39–44.

CHAPTER 6

1 Michael Korda, *Power!*.
2 Heidi Grant Halvorson, *No One Understands You,* (Kindle location 1211.)

3 J. Overbeck, B. Park, "When power does not corrupt: Superior individuation processes among powerful perceivers," *Journal of Personality and Social Psychology* 81, no. 4 (2001): 549–565.

4 To ride in the wake of a larger force with diminished resistance, as in: "In scaled wind-tunnel tests, driving 100 feet behind a semi at 55 mph will reduce drag on your car by 40%." https://www.treehugger.com/cars/drafting-behind-trucks-does-it-work.html (accessed 10/21/17)

5 Erving Goffman, *The Presentation of Self In Everyday Life.*

6 Robert I. Sutton, *The No Asshole Rule,* (Kindle location 778).

7 Jerry Useem, "Why It Pays to Be a Jerk."

8 Robert I. Sutton, *The No Asshole Rule,* (Kindle location 777).

9 Ibid., (Kindle location 261).

10 Adam Grant, *Give and Take,* 5.

11 R. Ruback, D. Juieng, "Territorial Defense in Parking Lots: Retaliation Against Waiting Drivers," *Journal of Applied Social Psychology* 27, no. 9 (1997): 821–834.

12 James W. Pennebaker, *The Secret Life of Pronouns: What Our Words Say About Us,* (Bloomsbury Press, 2011).

13 Ellen Langer experiment as quoted in *Magic Words* by Tim David, (Prentice Hall Press, 2014).

14 George Orwell, "Politics and the English Language," *Horizon*, GB London, 1946.

CHAPTER 7

1 Hervey M. Cleckley, *The Mask of Sanity,* 541.

2 A. Book, T. Methot, N. Gauthier, et al., "The Mask of Sanity Revisited: Psychopathic Traits and Affective Mimicry" *Evolutionary Psychological Science* 1: 91 2015).

3 William Shakespeare, *Macbeth.*

4 William March, *The Bad Seed* (Holt, Rinehard & Winston, 1954). Reprinted by Vinage Books 2015.

5 Andy McNab, Kevin Dutton, *The Good Psychopath's Guide to Success* (Transworld Publishers, 2014), 280.

6 Michael Korda, *Power!.*

7 S. Rick, S. Ross, M. Schweiter, "The Imbibing Idiot Bias: Consuming Alcohol Can Be Hazardous to Your (Perceived) Intelligence," *Journal of Consumer Psychology* (June 12, 2012).

8 Cindy Ocean, "Theater Acting Techniques," Quizlet: https://quizlet.com/177919538/theatre-acting-techniques-flash-cards/ (accessed March 2017).

9 Jonah Weiner, "Understanding James Franco" *Rolling Stone* 1258, April 7, 2016.

10 http://www.goodreads.com/quotes/36719-i-try-to-stay-in-a-constant-state-of-confusion.

11 Marlon Brando, foreword to *The Technique of Acting* by Stella Adler, (Bantam Books, 1988).

12 Truman Capote, *In Cold Blood* (Random House 1966).

13 Oliver P. John, Richard W. Robins, "Accuracy and bias in self-perception: Individual differences in self-enhancement and the role of narcissism," *Journal of Personality and Social Psychology* 66 no. 1 (1994): 206–219.

CHAPTER 8

1   Kirstin Weir, "The Power of Self Control," American Psychological Association: http://www.apa.org/monitor/2012/01/self-control.aspx (accessed April 2017).
2   Psyblog, "Does Familiarity Breed Liking or Contempt?" *Psyblog*: http://www.spring.org.uk/2011/09/does-familiarity-breed-liking-or-contempt.php (accessed April 2017).
3   Heidi Grant Halvorson, *No One Understands You*, (Kindle location 678.)
4   George Orwell, *Down and Out in Paris and London* (George Orwell, 1933). Reprinted by Houghton Mifflin Harcourt, 1972, 76.
5   NOTE: For professional security reasons, names have been omitted.
6   George Orwell, *Down and Out in Paris and London*, 79.
7   Adam Green, "A Pickpocket's Tale," *The New Yorker*, http://www.newyorker.com/magazine/2013/01/07/a-pickpockets-tale?mbid=nl (accessed March 2017).
8   Adam Gopnik, "The Real Work," *The New Yorker*, http://www.newyorker.com/magazine/2008/03/17/the-real-work?mbid=nl (accessed March 2017).
9   A. Mack, I. Rock, *Innatention Blindness* (MIT Press 1998).
10 S. Macknik, M. King, et al., "Attention and awareness in stage magic: turning tricks into research," *Nature Reviews*: http://www.nature.com/nrn/journal/v9/n11/full/nrn2473.html (accessed May 2017).
11 Ibid.
12 NOTE: terms coined by Goffman, Erving; described by me.
13 Robert I. Sutton, *The No Asshole Rule,* (Kindle location 1543).

CHAPTER 9

1   Robert Greene, *The Art of Seduction* (Penguin, 2001).
2   Richard H. Thaler, Cass R. Sunstein, *Nudge*, 33–34.
3   Ibid., 6.
4   Survey, "America's Top Fears 2016," Chapman University: https://blogs.chapman.edu/wilkinson/2016/10/11/americas-top-fears-2016/ (accessed February 2017).
5   Dan Lyons, *Disrupted*, 77.
6   James Fallon, *The Psychopath Inside,* 207.
7   Andy McNab, Kevin Dutton, *The Good Psychopath's Guide to Success,* 217.
8   Richard H. Thaler, Cass R. Sunstein, *Nudge,* 08.
9   Robert I. Sutton, *The No Asshole Rule,* (Kindle location 360).
10 Upton Sinclair, *I, Candidate for Governor: And How I Go Licked* (Farrar and Rinehart, 1935). Reprinted Berkeley: University of California Press, 1994.

CHAPTER 10

1   Jerry Useem, "Why It Pays to Be a Jerk."
2   Ibid.
3   James Fallon, *The Psychopath Inside*, 223.
4   Megan Garber, "It Pays to Be a Jerk, Bob Dylan Edition," *The Atlantic*, http://www.theatlantic.com/entertainment/archive/2016/11/it-pays-to-be-a-jerk-episode-4745-bob-dylan/507935/ (accessed December 2016.).
5   Michael Korda, *Power!*.
6   Laura Stampler, "The Bizarre History of Women's Clothing Sizes," *Time* magazine, http://time.com/3532014/women-clothing-sizes-history (accessed November 2016).

CHAPTER 11

1   Michael Korda, *Power!*.
2   Erving Goffman, *The Presentation of Self In Everyday Life*.
3   Harry G. Frankfurt, *On Bullshit* (Princeton University Press, 2005).
4   Staff, "Help Us Diagram This Sentence," *Slate*, http://www.slate.com/blogs/lexicon_valley/2015/07/31/donald_trump_this_run_on_sentence_from_a_speech_in_sun_city_south_carolina.html (accessed February 2017).
5   NOTE: A good idea, endorsed by high Machivellians in the experiment "Impressions of high and low Machiavellian Men" by Cherulnik P.; Way J.; Ames S.; Hutto, D. 1981.
6   Frank Kelly Rich, "How to Ace an Intervention," *Modern Drunkard*, http://www.drunkard.com/03-03_intervention/ (accessed January 2017).
7   Oliver James, *Office Politics: How to Thrive in a World of Lying, Backstabbing and Dirty Tricks,* (Vermilion, 2013), 3.
8   Erving Goffman, *The Presentation of Self in Everyday Life*.
9   Philip Houston, Michael Floyd, Susan Carnicero. *Spy the Lie* (St. Martin's Press, 2012) Paraphrased.
10   Ibid., (Kindle location 1132).
11   James W. Pennebaker, *The Secret Life of Pronouns*.
12   Mark Seal, "The Man In the Rockefeller Suit," *Vanity Fair*, http://www.vanityfair.com/style/2009/01/fake_rockefeller200901 (accessed February 2017).
13   Malcolm Gladwell. *Blink: The Power of Thinking Without Thinking* (Little, Brown And Company, 2005).
14   Stuart Chase, *Guides to Straight Thinking: With 13 Common Fallacies* (Harper, 1956).
15   Marina Krakovksy, "When Threats Are Better Than Anger," Stanford Business. https://www.gsb.stanford.edu/insights/when-threats-are-better-anger (accessed April 2017).
16   I. Lewis, B.Watson, R. Tay, K.M. White, "The role of fear appeals in improving driver safety: A review of the effectiveness of fear-arousing (threat) appeals in road safety advertising," *International Journal of Behavioral Consultation and Therapy* 3 no. 2 (2007): 203–222.

17   Sebastian Bailey, "The Psychological Tricks Behind Apple's Service Secrets," *Forbes*, https://www.forbes.com/sites/sebastianbailey/2012/09/11/the-psychological-tricks-behind-apples-service-secrets-2/#55f66dd2124e (accessed April 2017).

CHAPTER 12

1   Tzu, Sun, *The Art of War*.
2   *The WEEK*, 16 no. 797 (November 18, 2016).
3   Staff. "What Does Putin Want?" *The Week*, http://theweek.com/articles/672835/what-does-putin-want (accessed Ferbruary 2017).
4   Olivia Goldhill, "A Philosopher's 350-Year-Old-Trick . . . ," Quartz Media, https://qz.com/778767/to-tell-someone-theyre-wrong-first-tell-them-how-theyre-right/?utm_source=kwfb&kwp_0=338025&kwp_4=1289586&kwp_1=573529 (accessed November 2016).
5   Andrew Higgins, "Foes of Russia Say Child Pornography is Planted to Ruin Them," *The New York Times*, https://www.nytimes.com/2016/12/09/world/europe/vladimir-putin-russia-fake-news-hacking-cybersecurity.html?_r=0 (accessed December 2016).
6   Patrick Hamilton, "Gas Light," 1939. Published in the USA as "Angel Street: A Victorian Thriller in Three Acts," A Samuel French Acting Edition, 1942, (Kindle location 570).

CHAPTER 13

1   P. Babiak, R. Hare, *Snakes in Suits,* 88.
2   Robert D. Hare, Without Conscience, 65.

CHAPTER 14

1   Jerry Useem, "Why It Pays to Be a Jerk."
2   Geoffrey Sonnabend, as quoted in *The Museum of Jurassic Technology Jubilee Catalogue,* Society for the Diffusion of Useful Information Press, 2002.
3   K. Fujita; S. Itakura. Diversity of Cognitions; Evolution, Development, Domestication, Pathology (Kyoto University Press, 2006), 303.
4   Daniel L. Schacter, *Seven Sins of Memory, How the Mind Forgets and Remembers.* Houghton Mifflin. 2001. Terminology from him, descriptions by me.
5   Susan Krauss Whitbourne, "Happiness: It's all About the Ending." Psychology Today.   https://www.psychologytoday.com/blog/fulfillment-any-age/201209/happiness-it-s-all-about-the-ending (accessed May 2017).
6   Richard Dawkins, "Viruses of the Mind"; *Dennett and His Critics: Demystifying Mind.* Blackwell Publishers. 1993.
7   Stanley Cohen, *Folk Devils and Moral Panics.* 1972. Republished by Routledge, 2011.
8   Christopher Bucktin, "Meet Pablo Escobar's Hitman." http://www.mirror.co.uk/news/world-news/meet-pablo-escobars-hitman-worlds-8857026 (accessed January 2017). Emphasis, mine.

9   Harriet Aexander, "How 'Popeye' became Pablo Escobar's Favourite Hitman. *The Telegraph*. http://www.telegraph.co.uk/news/worldnews/southamerica/ colombia/11058550/How-Popeye-became-Pablo-Escobars-favourite-hitman. html (accessed January 2017).

10 Arturo Wallace, "Drug Boss Pablo Escobar Still Divides Colombia," BBC News, http://www.bbc.com/news/world-latin-america-25183649 (accessed January 2017).

11 Isabel Vincent, "Pablo Escobar's Son Says His Dad's Death Was By Suicide," *The New York Post*, http://nypost.com/2016/08/14/pablo-escobars-son-says-his-dads-death-was-by-suicide/ (accessed May 2017).

12 David Agren, "El Chapo Capture: Mexico Drug Lord's 'Desire to Make Biopic' Helped Agents Find Him," *The Guardian*, https://www.theguardian.com/ world/2016/jan/09/el-chapo-capture-mexico-drug-lords-desire-to-make-biopic-helped-agents-find-him, (accessed February 2017).

EPILOGUE

1   American Psychiatry Association. *Diagnostic and Statistical Manual of Mental Disorders, Fifth Edition*. Arlington VA. American Psychiatric Association, 2013: 693.